THE MIND GAME

GAINING A PSYCHOLOGICAL EDGE
IN FANTASY PREMIER LEAGUE

ROSS DOWSETT

HALCYON

PUBLISHING

Published by Halcyon Publishing

First published 2021

Edited by Adam Bushby & Rob MacDonald

ISBN: 978-1-9196-2400-6

Cover design by Peter Rowson
Layout by Rob MacDonald

For my fiancée and my family

Praise for The Mind Game

"Ross has a knack for making complex psychological theories both understandable and relatable to our efforts as FPL managers. This book helps to identify faulty decision-making processes, giving you an extra tool to get ahead of the pack."

Chaz Phillips – @FFScout_Az
(3x Top 5k Finishes | PhD in Psychology)

"Engaging and insightful, Ross condenses his deep academic understanding of how our mind works into a series of practical tips for FPL. We can all learn something from this book!"

Joshua Bull – @JoshuaABull
(2019/20 FPL Champion)

"Managing yourself is just as important, if not more important than managing your team. Reading this fantastic book will give you a much better chance of achieving FPL success."

Mark McGettigan – @FPLGeneral
(3x Top 500 Finishes)

"Understanding what drives our decision-making can help us all become better FPL managers; Ross has written the How To guide."

Mark Sutherns – @FFScout_Mark
(4x Top 500 Finishes | Founder of FFScout)

Contents

About the author   9

Acknowledgements   11

Introduction   13

Part One: Pre-Gameweek Research   17

Introduction to Part One   19

Chapter 1: Digesting FPL content   21

Chapter 2: The dark side of social media   31

Chapter 3: The fear of missing out   39

Chapter 4: Conducting your own FPL research   47

Chapter 5: Rejecting new information – closed-mindedness   53

Part Two: Making Your FPL Decisions   57

Introduction to Part Two   59

Chapter 6: Gut feeling – can we trust it?   61

Chapter 7: Risk-taking in FPL   77

Chapter 8: When should we make FPL decisions?   83

Chapter 9: Decision-making in the context of transfers
and captaincy   95

Chapter 10: The psychology of being a fan   103

Chapter 11: The 90 minutes following the FPL deadline   107

Part Three: Post-Gameweek Reflections   **111**

Introduction to Part Three   113

Chapter 12: Post-gameweek evaluations – how did I do?   115

Chapter 13: Psychological advice for coping
with negative outcomes   121

Chapter 14: Looking forward to the next gameweek   131

Part Four:
The Psychology Behind Your Chip Strategy   **135**

Introduction to Part Four   137

Chapter 15: Wildcard and Free Hit   139

Chapter 16: Delayed gratification – can you wait?   141

Part Five: Conclusions   **149**

Chapter 17: My top five psychological tips   151

Chapter 18: Enjoy the wonderful game of FPL   155

End of book tasks and practical help   157

About the author

Ross Dowsett is a BSc Psychology and MSc Sport Psychology graduate, finishing as valedictorian (top of his year) at both levels. He is currently completing a PhD in Sport Psychology, exploring the role of virtual reality in accelerating skill acquisition. Alongside this, Ross is lecturing BSc Sport Science students in Statistics and Sport Psychology.

Since June 2020, Ross has been applying the psychological concepts and theories discussed in this book to Fantasy Premier League (FPL) on Twitter (@FPL__Raptor) and as an author for FPL Connect, a popular website for FPL content. The first of his articles explored the phenomenon known as 'fear of missing out', which is discussed in Chapter 3 of this book. Since then, Ross has continued to explore multiple psychological concepts, spanning the fields of Cognitive Psychology, Social Psychology, Sport Psychology and Behavioural Economics.

Ross has a sporting background of his own, playing youth football for Tottenham Hotspur from the age of seven to 15. This is where his passion for football began and where many of his ideas for research originate.

Acknowledgements

Writing this book has been an incredibly challenging yet rewarding journey. I could not have imagined how one project could completely consume every part of my being for an entire year, but I have loved every second of it.

For anyone that has written a book, you will know that it is not possible without support from those around you. I would like to thank my incredible family, in particular my mum and dad. Without your support, I would never have been able to attend university and gain the education and experience which has allowed me to write this book. You have never stopped believing in me and I would not be where I am today without you both.

Thank you to my big sister, Hayley, for always supporting me. You were always there for me, putting me on a pedestal and supporting me through school. You have always been my rock and I feel privileged to call you my sister. Thank you to my nan, Shirley, for always being the first to congratulate me on my achievements and always being my biggest fan. Thank you to my brother-in-law, Luke, for being a brilliant FPL rival and pushing me to become a better manager.

I would also like to say thank you to the love of life, my fiancée, Camille. You have been the silent heroine, responsible for much of what makes this book what it is. You inspired many of the ideas which this book is built upon; you helped craft the title and front cover; you proofread and edited the book to a professional standard; and you supported me while I spent countless nights writing into the early hours. I truly could not have done this without you. I am eternally grateful.

Thank you to Simon Jones and Karan Thorat for your friendship and trusted opinion throughout this entire process. Whether it be allowing me to explain my new ideas, or giving your invaluable opinions on different aspects of the book, I appreciate you both very much.

Finally, thank you to Gianni Butticè and Toby Margetts for providing me with invaluable advice as I began the journey of writing this book, and also putting me in touch with the amazing publishers responsible for making it happen, Rob MacDonald and Adam Bushby. Thank you both for believing in my concept and for working tirelessly with me to turn it from a dream into reality. Thank you for your honesty and integrity throughout this process – I am very glad that I met you both.

Introduction

Fantasy Premier League (FPL) has transcended its role as a virtual game, developing into a culture, community and a way of life for many of us. It delights, angers, torments, shocks and consumes us – and let's be honest, we love it! We love the highs, we despise the lows, but every year we cannot help but approach the first week of the Premier League season and think: "This could be my year". When FPL is going smoothly, there is no better feeling in the world. The euphoria and pride associated with a successful decision, week or season is unrivalled. The pure jubilation of a captaincy haul, a green arrow or destroying our mini-league rival is what we live for. We want more of it. We cannot get enough of it. As such, we continue to search for innovative ways to improve our success in the game. We find a new podcast, a new website, a new underlying statistic that may give us that subtle edge over our family, friends and colleagues.

This book is the latest addition to this increasingly crowded field, but it is not like anything you will have read before. I truly believe it can transform the way you play, forever.

> *"Give a man a fish, and you feed him for a day. Teach a man to fish, and you feed him for a lifetime."*

While this passage has become somewhat of a cliché over time, it perfectly encompasses the purpose of this book. There is no doubt that there are multiple benefits to weekly pieces of advice, such as 'captain X player' and 'transfer out Y player', however, this is ultimately a limited approach. Do you know why you are choosing that player? Are you able to evaluate your decision and improve the next time you face a similar scenario?

What could you have done differently? This book can provide you with the tools to improve the manner in which you make decisions, which will allow you to make optimal decisions yourself. You will learn how to identify your own management style, your strengths, your weaknesses and, in doing so, approach FPL in a more effective manner. Learning who you are within the world of FPL and where there is still room for improvement, will ultimately set you apart from the rest.

Beyond FPL, this book will encourage you to think critically about the manner in which you approach key decisions in life and whether or not your decision-making could be further fine-tuned. You will learn things about yourself that you have perhaps never even considered, delve into the deepest parts of your mind and come out the other side a more knowledgeable and well-equipped individual. This is more than just a book about FPL, this is a book which will allow you to gain a deeper understanding of yourself.

We will also tackle the most important element of FPL – enjoyment. How can we deal with negative outcomes in FPL? Is there a way to ensure we play this game with fun at the forefront? Is there a gold standard technique for avoiding feeling down after a bad gameweek? If you finish bottom of your mini-league each year or outside of the top 1 million, but you are truly enjoying playing FPL, I believe you are the real winner.

Notes about the structure of the book

This book has been organised according to the weekly structure of FPL, with each part covering a different phase of the cycle:

Part 1: Pre-Gameweek Research

Part 2: Making your FPL Decisions

Part 3: Post-Gameweek Reflections

Part 4: The Psychology Behind Your Chip Strategy

Part 5: Conclusions

The hope is that this book will guide you through the week and allow you to focus on each phase of the game before moving on to the next. You can then return to the book for advice at specific time points throughout the season after your initial read-through. In addition to the information and my personal application of the research to FPL, many of the chapters include questionnaires, tasks and tools to allow you to interact with the content.

This book will include references to multiple psychological articles, all of which will be cited and referenced according to the American Psychological Association (APA) format, the standard for publishing psychological work in the UK. All of the psychological articles cited in the main text (in brackets) can be found at the end of the book in the References section, should you wish to explore the topic in greater detail. Further, while all technical and psychological terminology will be discussed in-text, there is also a glossary at the end of the book, should you wish to re-address a specific concept.

Alongside the psychological glossary, there is an FPL glossary should you require elaboration on any terminology used throughout the book. While every attempt has been made to correctly interpret and describe the relevant literature and concepts, the application of this research to FPL is subjective and should be taken as an educated opinion as opposed to factual.

P◆RT ONE

PRE-GAMEWEEK RESEARCH

Introduction to Part One

The largest portion of the standard FPL week is spent preparing for upcoming gameweeks. Within this, there are a multitude of ways we can aid preparation: in-person discussions; social media interactions; conducting our own analysis; listening to podcasts; reading articles; watching videos; re-watching the games and much more.

Unfortunately, when preparing for an upcoming gameweek, we are vulnerable to an array of psychological processes that may result in us making ineffective decisions and mistakes that we ultimately regret. The goal in this first section is to provide you with the relevant knowledge to identify these problems before they occur, and the relevant tools to deal with them before they develop. This should allow you to prepare for each upcoming gameweek in the optimal fashion and consequently, make the most effective decisions possible.

Chapter 1:
Digesting FPL content

This first chapter of this book tackles the issues that may arise with digesting FPL content produced by other FPL managers. Indeed, as 'serious' managers we spend a lot of time reading articles and threads from other managers, listening to our favourite podcasts, or watching our favourite video creators. This allows us to buy players and adopt approaches that perhaps we would not have considered alone. The great managers will acknowledge the abundance of quality content that is available to them, but the very *best* managers will know how to integrate this with their own knowledge and decision-making.

Within this chapter, I will introduce you to one of the main themes of this book: cognitive biases. As FPL managers, it is vitally important to be masters of our own minds. We must find ways to improve the effectiveness of our decision-making and, in doing so, propel ourselves up the rankings and beat our mini-league rivals. One way of doing this is by being aware of, and learning to control, our cognitive biases.

Cognitive biases

Cognitive bias is the umbrella term used to describe the tendency for us to perceive information based on our own experiences and prior beliefs, which can result in the distortion of information, unreasonable or inaccurate interpretation, and flawed decision-making. In other words, the process by which objective information is interpreted subjectively and often inaccurately. The discovery of cognitive biases by Tversky and Kahneman (1974) resulted in a large cohort of literature exploring the topic.

Prior to this, we believed that humans were always driven by rules of logic and probability, contributing to rational thinking (Lieder, Griffiths, Huys, & Goodman, 2018), when in fact, the very existence of cognitive biases suggests that we are subject to irrational and biased cognitive processes, that can potentially result in sub-optimal reasoning and decision-making. In other words, cognitive biases show us that we are not perfect!

Within the overarching term 'cognitive bias', there are multiple sub-biases. There are hundreds of cognitive biases explored in current psychological research, however, in this book, we will cover 28 of those most applicable to FPL. Before we begin, I would like to draw your attention to the most ironic cognitive bias of all – the **bias blind spot**. The bias blind spot is the cognitive bias of recognising the impact of biases on the judgement of others, while failing to see the impact of biases on one's own judgement – we are blind to our own biases! Pronin, Lin and Ross (2002) refer to this as an 'asymmetry in perceived susceptibility to biases'. That is, we think we are shielded from, and less susceptible to, the very biases that we highlight in other individuals.

The bias blind spot is demonstrated in a number of studies. For example, Pronin et al. (2002) conducted a series of experiments whereby they asked Stanford University students to rate their susceptibility to biases in relation to other groups. The authors found that the students rated themselves significantly less susceptible to suffering from cognitive biases than: a) the average American; b) the average fellow classmate; c) the average airport traveller (i.e., a stranger). However, the authors did not stop there, as they demonstrated that not only were the participants unable to identify their own biases, they were also largely unaware they were suffering from the blind spot.

The authors demonstrated this by asking participants to rate themselves on six personality dimensions (three positive and three negative) in relation to other Stanford University students. For example, they were asked to rate how considerate they were of others, ranging from 'much less than the average Stanford student' to 'much more than the average Stanford student'.

After rating themselves in relation to their fellow students, the participants were given a piece of paper with the following description and asked to read it:

Studies have shown that on the whole, people show a 'better than average' effect when assessing themselves relative to other members within their group. That is, 70-80% of individuals consistently rate themselves 'better than average' on qualities that they perceive as positive and, conversely, evaluate themselves as having 'less than average' amounts of characteristics they believe are negative.

Participants were then asked to return to their answers and indicate whether an objective resource (with no bias) would give the same response as them. In other words, were their responses objectively accurate? Of the 79 participants that claimed a 'better-than-average' status, only 19 (24%) indicated that their responses had been biased. Sixty-three percent claimed that they were entirely accurate, while 13% claimed that they were actually being too modest! Therefore, even after the participants had their attention explicitly drawn to the fact that they may have been biased, less than a quarter were actually able to spot this in themselves.

This research is important as it demonstrates that as individuals we struggle to identify biases in our thoughts and behaviour. Being aware of our difficulty to reflect introspectively (i.e., examining our own thoughts and behaviours) will improve our chances of catching our own biases and refraining from making decisions in a sub-optimal fashion.

It is also worth noting that as you work your way through this book, you may be unable to spot these biases in your own thoughts and behaviours. If you think 'I don't do that', or 'I am not prone to making that mistake', you may be demonstrating the bias blind spot.

The order in which we receive information

It is vitally important to consider the order in which we receive information, both in relation to FPL content and FPL data. That is, if you consume multiple pieces of content throughout the week, these will be consumed in a specific order. There will be pieces of information you consume at the start of the week and pieces you consume towards the end. This may have been something that you have not given any thought to, but the order in which you receive this information is actually vital with regard to which pieces you adopt and integrate, and which pieces are forgotten.

The best place to begin is with the first piece of content we digest. **Anchoring bias** suggests that we favour the first piece of information we learn on a given topic, hence the idea of an 'anchor'. In one of the original experiments demonstrating the anchoring bias, participants were split into two groups and given five seconds to estimate a sum:

Group A: 1 x 2 x 3 x 4 x 5 x 6 x 7 x 8

Group B: 8 x 7 x 6 x 5 x 4 x 3 x 2 x 1

The more astute readers will notice immediately that these two equations are identical in their sum total, but reversed in their ordering – the correct answer for both sums is 40,320. However, in this experiment, the median (average) estimate for Group A was 512, whereas the median estimate for Group B was 2,250 (Tversky & Kahneman, 1974). Due to people utilising heuristics (mental shortcuts) and often only processing the initial pieces of information to the fullest extent, group A massively under-estimated the total sum.

In another experiment carried out to demonstrate the anchoring bias, participants were asked to estimate various quantities in percentages – for example, "What percentage of African countries are in the U.N?" (Tversky & Kahneman, 1974). After the question, a 'wheel of fortune' was spun in the presence of the participant, landing on a number between 0-100, for example, 65(%). The participants were then asked to state whether this number was too high or too low and then reach their estimate by moving upward or downward from the number on the wheel. Importantly, they were informed that the initial number on the wheel was arbitrary and had no relationship with the correct answer. Group A received 10% as their starting point from the wheel and Group B received 65% as their starting point from the wheel. The median (average) estimate of the percentage of African countries in the U.N. for Group A was 25% and for Group B was 45%. Therefore, the original arbitrary number that participants were presented with cognitively biased their subsequent estimate.

The concept of anchoring bias is closely correlated with the **serial position effect** (also known as the **primacy-recency effect**). Serial position effect explains the tendency for individuals to remember information presented at the beginning of a list (primacy effect) and the end of a list (recency effect), more so than the information in the middle of the list (Atkinson &

Shiffrin, 1968). However, this bias extends far beyond lists to all aspects of decision-making that rely on memory. Things that are presented at the beginning and end are often remembered most accurately.

(As a side tip, if you are ever offered the opportunity to choose the time of day that you interview for a job, choose the very early morning or the late afternoon. In the middle of the day you may be forgotten due to the serial position effect!).

The real question, though, is 'how does this apply to FPL?'. The above two biases are perhaps most explicit at the beginning of the season, when we make hundreds of drafts for the new FPL campaign. It is most likely that when you decide on your final team before Gameweek 1, you will have a large majority of players from your initial few teams (anchoring bias and primacy effect), and also a large number of players from your latest drafts (recency effect), but will ignore and/or forget players from the middle 20-30% of your drafts.

It is also particularly applicable when researching which players to captain and transfer, i.e. when you digest content created by the FPL Community. Imagine a scenario where you read an article which suggests captaining Raheem Sterling for the double gameweek. It may be that you tie your metaphorical anchor to this idea and end up making it your final choice. Alternatively, it may be that you read the article shortly before the deadline, which unwittingly convinces you to disregard all of your prior research.

My advice here, therefore, is to make sure you have considered all of the available options when making your decision, ensuring you do not succumb to anchoring bias or the serial-position effect. You can take this one step further and note down all of the options and possible decisions you have considered, so that you can refer back to them physically without the possibility of disregarding them in place of initial or recent alternatives.

Pitfalls to be aware of when digesting FPL content

The very fact that you are reading this book is a sign that you enjoy digesting content provided by content creators and members of the FPL community. However, while reading, listening and watching FPL content, as well as the order of the information, there are a couple of key cognitive biases that we must be aware of. The first of these is **belief bias**.

Belief bias refers to the tendency to evaluate the validity of an argument based on the plausibility of the conclusion (Markovits & Nantel, 1989). In other words, if the conclusion is convincing and/or aligned with a belief that we already hold, we are likely to agree with the entire argument, irrespective of the quality of the content of the argument.

Here, I have provided a fictional Twitter thread to demonstrate an example of belief bias. In this fictional scenario, imagine that you approach the Gameweek 15 deadline with Vardy as your favourite captaincy choice.

 [Thread on Captaincy for GW15]

In this thread, I will compare the underlying statistics for the main three captaincy options: Salah, Rashford and Vardy, and I will also explore the underlying statistics for the defences of the teams they are facing.

Let's do this! (1/5)

 Salah (£12.5m)

Salah currently ranks 6th in the league for expected goals (2.65) over the last 5 gameweeks. He also ranks 9th in the league for shots in the box (12).

His opponents, Burnley, rank 20th for expected goals conceded (13.51), 19th for shots conceded (38). (2/5)

 Rashford (£9.5m)

Rashford currently ranks 12th in the league for expected goals (1.31) over the last 5 gameweeks. He also ranks 15th for shots in the box (7).

His opponents, Villa, rank 12th for expected goals conceded (7.54) and 9th for shots conceded (19). (3/5)

Vardy (£10.0m) 🥅

Vardy currently ranks 2nd in the league for expected goals (2.98) over the last 5 gameweeks. He also ranks 1st for shots in the box (16).

His opponents, West Ham, rank 3rd for expected goals conceded (2.84) and 5th for shots conceded (12). (4/5)

 CONCLUSION! 🥅

There is absolutely NO DOUBT that Vardy is the best captaincy option. His own underlying statistics are the best in the league, and we all know that when Vardy is in form, there is no stopping him!

Everything points towards a Vardy party this weekend! (5/5)

I want you to consider a few things about this thread. Does this agree with your already established preference? *Yes.* Is the conclusion convincing? *Yes.* Does the conclusion accurately portray the research and information in the thread? *Not quite.*

Yes, according to these statistics, Jamie Vardy is in the best individual form. However, there is no discussion as to the great form of his opponents, West Ham. Further, while Jamie Vardy is second for expected goals (2.98) and first for shots in the box (16), and Salah is sixth (2.65) and ninth (12) respectively, there is actually not a massive difference between the numbers. Yes, Salah is sixth and ninth, but with only 0.33 lower expected goals than Vardy, and four fewer shots in the box. The magnitude of the difference in the underlying statistics of Salah and Vardy is smaller than it perhaps looks at a first glance.

Also, I would personally be thinking: "Who is first in the league for expected goals, if Vardy is second and 'the best captaincy option'?" Of course, this is only a fictional thread, but you will see lots of content whereby the conclusion is incredibly convincing and aligns with your prior views, but does not necessarily follow on from the main body or consider all of the options.

My key advice here is to not skip to the end of an article or Twitter thread and read the conclusion before reading the body of the content. Further, before reading the conclusion, ask yourself what you would conclude based on the bulk of the content: "Given what this content creator has stated, what would I conclude is the best decision to make?"

Often, the conclusion will not be entirely aligned with the actual content, or will be more convincing than the evidence suggests. On Twitter, this can of course be even more drastic, with the use of emojis and GIFs further sensationalising an otherwise regular conclusion. It is always good practice to think critically and to arrive at your own conclusions wherever possible.

The second bias to consider while digesting FPL content is the FPL favourite – **confirmation bias**. Confirmation bias is the tendency to search for, interpret and utilise information in a fashion that confirms, supports and reinforces our already-established beliefs and preferences (Nickerson, 1998). The most commonly-used example to demonstrate this concept is in medical practice (Groopman, 2007, as cited in Gray, 2011). Imagine a situation whereby a doctor is examining a patient presenting symptoms. Without being able to control this, a doctor will often form a quick hypothesis about the cause of the symptoms, that is, their initial diagnosis without running any tests. After forming this initial hypothesis, the doctor may then search for evidence which confirms this belief, rejecting or overlooking information which does not fit their expectations or refutes their hypothesis. This can often result in a misdiagnosis and an incorrect treatment plan.

In an ideal world, doctors (and all humans) should actively search for information that disconfirms their prior beliefs. By looking for information that refutes our initial ideas and beliefs, we are more likely to find the objectively correct decision and outcome.

In FPL, confirmation bias is applicable both in the search for content and the processing of content. Imagine a scenario whereby we want to captain Marcus Rashford, but do not have the data or logic to support this decision. As a result, we turn to one of the many platforms for FPL content and search through until we find an article, podcast or video which discusses Rashford as the best captaincy option and we think to ourselves, "Ah, see, I knew Rashford was the best captaincy option". This is confirmation bias.

We are actively searching for content which supports our desire to captain Rashford and, quite possibly, ignoring all of the other data which discuss and suggest captaining other players. Further, it also ties in nicely with the aforementioned belief bias, in that we will often accept the conclusion of the content without critically assessing the actual research, purely as it confirms the decision we wanted to make anyway! In any case, always attempt to evaluate the research and content objectively and acknowledge any preconceived preferences you may have before digesting content.

Chapter 2:
The dark side of social media

As well as considering how the direct consumption of content will affect our decision-making, we must also consider the medium through which the majority of content is produced and discussed – that being, social media. The best thing about FPL for many (myself included) is the FPL Community. We have the opportunity to discuss the beautiful game (and the virtual version) with interesting, diverse individuals. We have quick access to an array of content and tools created by numerous brilliant managers across the world. We are encouraged to build relationships and friendships that last for many years, and we do all of this as part of a collective community.

However, the very fact that we are part of a community means that we cannot just consider ourselves as individuals, we must also consider how we interact with, and function within, the larger group. As highlighted by Raafat, Chater and Frith (2009), "we are all embedded in a complex system of social structures, which ground and organise much of our behaviour" (p. 420).

In this chapter, we will explore the various 'group psychology' constructs at play when interacting with the FPL Community on social media platforms. As Twitter is the social media platform with the largest community – and the platform that I utilise the most – a lot of the examples used in this chapter will apply directly to Twitter. However, these concepts can be applied to all social media platforms and, to some extent, interactions in everyday life. Even if you do not take part in the FPL discussions on social media, there is still a lot to be learnt in this chapter.

The positives of social media – the human need to belong

Before we discuss the 'dark-side' of social media, it is important to note that our interaction and engagement on social media serves as an important method for satisfying our human need to 'belong'. Baumeister and Leary (1995) explain that humans have "a pervasive drive to form and maintain at least a minimum quantity of lasting, positive and impactful interpersonal relationships" (p. 497).

Further, in **Maslow's Hierarchy of Needs** (see below), the need to belong is the third need that must be met on the journey to self-actualisation (Maslow, 1943). In other words, forming relationships and belonging to groups, such as the FPL Community, is an important step in realising our full potential and leading a happy and healthy life.

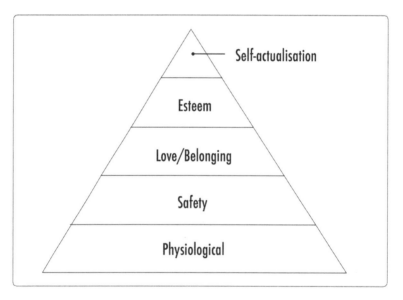

Therefore, I will not advise that FPL interactions on social media should be avoided, especially given the largely positive nature of the FPL Community. Social media can help satisfy our desire to be involved in social interactions and relationships. For many, interactions on social media (particularly those pertaining to FPL) can serve as an escape from the many problems we experience in everyday life. However, we must be aware of some key psychological effects and intrinsic biases, otherwise we could fall victim to the 'dark side' of social media.

The social media 'bubble'

For FPL, the social media bubble phenomenon is perhaps most applicable to the Twitter platform. In this context, the concept of a social media bubble corresponds to the perception that Twitter is representative of a larger amount of the active FPL managers than it actually is, giving the impression that the information and discussions we see on Twitter are indicative of the general consensus across FPL.

It is hard to estimate how many FPL accounts there are on Twitter. Some of the most popular accounts have begun to push over 150,000 followers. However, many of these will be inactive or will not discuss FPL. In fact, I would estimate that only approximately 50,000 (maximum estimate) of those accounts will regularly discuss FPL. Taking the figures from the 2020/21 season, there were over 8,000,000 teams. Assuming that some FPL managers have created multiple teams, let us be conservative and half that to 4,000,000 as a rough estimate of how many FPL managers there are.

Therefore, as a very rough estimate, we have 50,000 FPL accounts on Twitter and 4,000,000 FPL managers in total. This would suggest that Twitter only represents approximately 1.25% of FPL managers. If we take our estimates to the extremes in both directions, we can estimate that Twitter FPL accounts constitute between 0.25% and 7.5% of FPL managers.

The important message here is that social media can create a bubble around us, whereby we think that it is fully representative of the entirety of the game we play. That could not be further from the truth! Even as the community begins to grow and the official FPL begins to knuckle down on the creation of multiple teams, I do not expect platforms such as Twitter to constitute more than 10-15% of total managers that play the game. Therefore, do not be fooled into believing that everything you see on social media represents the general consensus, beliefs and decisions of the wider FPL manager base.

Herd mentality and groupthink

The two most common group psychology concepts that are prevalent on social media are **herd mentality** and **groupthink**. These two concepts are often used interchangeably as they stem from similar psychological theories and result in similar behavioural outcomes.

Herd mentality is a widely-discussed phenomenon which explains the process by which an individual's behaviour or beliefs align to that of the majority in the community to which they belong (Kameda & Hastie, 2015; Raafat et al., 2009). This coordination of opinions and decisions within the 'herd' is amplified by social interactions (i.e., through social media platforms). This is because the very nature of social media allows mass conformity and the ability to see a large group of people agreeing on one opinion or option.

In relation to FPL Twitter, herd mentality would describe an instance where an FPL manager internalises the view of the FPL community as their own belief and, as such, decides to conform to the mass decision. In other words, they are making a decision they would perhaps not make on their own and adopting the mentality of the herd instead.

Groupthink is a psychological phenomenon that occurs when the desire to maintain harmony within a community results in the group failing to realistically appraise an idea and come up with logical alternatives (Janis, 1971). Groupthink can produce truly disastrous results when taken to the extreme. In a real-life example, in 1986 NASA succumbed to the effects of groupthink in the Challenger Space Shuttle disaster. The orbiter 'Challenger' exploded only 73 seconds after launch, killing all seven crew members instantly.

How did a team of experts at NASA allow this catastrophe to occur? The answer is groupthink. One of the most important structural elements of the Challenger was a rubber part known as an 'O-ring'. This specific part is well known for being very sensitive to cold temperatures, only working effectively above 53 degrees. The temperature on the launchpad that morning was 36 degrees and, therefore, the team of engineers at NASA knew that there was a high risk of malfunction.

However, there was a large amount of national pressure on the team to stick to schedule with the launch and so despite a few of the engineers realising that there could be a major issue, rather than speaking up and stopping the launch, they kept quiet in an attempt to maintain harmony and stay in agreement with the leading figures. As a result of this, seven people lost their lives. If you would like to learn more about this incident, there are multiple videos and articles detailing the event online.

While in FPL the stakes are significantly lower than the Challenger disaster, this striking example does two things. Firstly, it demonstrates that groupthink is a very powerful process that has the opportunity to cause sub-optimal decision-making with potentially deadly consequences. Secondly, it demonstrates that many of the concepts we discuss in this book can be applied beyond FPL, to everyday life and important moments in history.

The most common example of groupthink in FPL is when the community decides on the best captaincy option for an upcoming gameweek and rather than suggest alternatives and appraise whether this is the best decision, the majority of FPL accounts will conform to the group decision and 'jump on the bandwagon' ('bandwagon' is a term used to describe a sudden increase in popularity of a specific asset).

An example of the **bandwagon effect** in a previous season was the Duffy-gate incident in 2019. In Double Gameweek 34 of the 2018/19 season, Shane Duffy (ex-Brighton CB) had a double gameweek of Bournemouth (H) and Cardiff (H). After weeks of discussion on social media, and many accounts touting him as the best option, Shane Duffy (£4.8m) was captained by a remarkably high 22.72% of managers in the top 10,000. Brighton went on to lose 5-0 to Bournemouth and 2-0 to Cardiff, with Duffy receiving a grand total of 1 point.

The question is: would the 22.72% of managers have captained Duffy without the influence of social media and without the processes of herd mentality and groupthink? Was a CB for a relegation-battling team the best choice, in a week where Spurs faced Huddersfield and Leicester faced Newcastle? Either way, you can see how we can quickly internalise the views of the community and our desire to maintain harmony and stick with the majority can result in some questionable group decisions.

You can also probably see why the terms herd mentality and groupthink are often used interchangeably. Essentially, the essence of the two concepts is that the individual either consciously or subconsciously internalises the view of the majority, either as the result of majority influence (herd mentality) or an intentional desire to avoid disrupting the harmony within the community (groupthink). In FPL, this results in adhering to the mass decision, bandwagons and quick rises in ownership.

Assuming that we would like to make our own decisions and avoid succumbing to following the masses, what can we do to avoid herd mentality and groupthink?

- Where possible, log off of social media and make your transfer/captaincy decisions without the input and pressure from the community.

- Try to avoid (where possible) running polls and constantly seeking opinions on your team – otherwise, you will likely succumb to herd mentality. If you ask which choice you should make, the herd/masses will likely convince you to follow their decisions.

- Seek multiple sources of information when making decisions. Use the community, use your gut feeling, use statistics, use the eye-test. This will limit your ability to be heavily influenced by a singular source, such as Twitter.

- Do not be afraid to stand out! Make decisions that challenge the status quo as this will add variety to the game and encourage other people to avoid herd mentality.

- Do not be afraid to challenge and question 'popular' opinions! Ask people why they have made certain transfer moves. Challenge people's captaincy choices and explain your differing opinion (but PLEASE do so in a positive manner).

Doing all of the above will limit your vulnerability to herd mentality and groupthink, and will also encourage others to be more individualistic and make decisions on their own accord. I would like to finish with an excellent quote from Albert Einstein, which takes a slightly exaggerative and satirical approach to the above concepts:

"When we all think alike, no one thinks very much."

Group polarisation

As well as heavily influencing the content of our decisions (i.e., what we actually decide to do), groups and communities on social media are capable of influencing our decisions to make them significantly more extreme. This is a phenomenon known as **group polarisation**. Group polarisation refers to the tendency for groups to shift toward more extreme decisions following group interaction, as well as the natural inclination for groups to reach more extreme decisions than an individual (Lamm, 1988).

It is important to note that group polarisation only intensifies the position/opinion already held by the majority of the group members (Jones & Roleosfma, 2000). Therefore, group polarisation will not cause the group to come up with a crazy and outlandish idea, it will simply reinforce and amplify the view already held by the majority. For example, if there are murmurings of captaining a differential option for a gameweek by multiple members of the community, group discussions and interactions on Twitter are likely to amplify these murmurings and polarise them, making it shift from a small possibility to the most obvious choice.

So what should we do about group polarisation in relation to FPL on social media? There are a couple of pieces of advice I can give which overlap with some of the aforementioned social psychology concepts:

1. If you spot an extreme or questionable mass decision in the community, attempt to make sense of it logically and seek out information to question, challenge and improve this view. Do NOT just accept the decision as correct.

2. Attempt to play 'devil's advocate' and explore reasons why this extreme decision may not be the most advisable. This will lead to people being less likely to succumb to polarisation.

The common knowledge effect

The last psychological concept we will look at in this chapter is the common knowledge effect, which is a fairly under-appreciated part of group psychology. This concept describes the tendency for group members to only share and discuss information that is common knowledge between multiple group members and to not bring unique knowledge to the discussion (Stasser & Titus, 1985).

This is represented and explained by a fantastic task that can be perfectly applied to FPL, called the 'Hidden Profile Task'. In the Hidden Profile Task, information that is made public to the entire group will point to Option A being better. However, Option B is instead the objective 'better' choice, but the pieces of evidence that support Option B are only shown to an individual member – they are not common knowledge. To summarise, Option A appears better to the entire group, however, one member has knowledge that shows Option B is better.

In these situations, the group will spend the majority of the time reviewing and discussing the facts that suggest that Option A is better (as this is the common knowledge) and, as such, never discover the limitations of Option A and the benefits of option B (Stasser & Titus, 1987). Worryingly, Lu, Yuan & McLeod (2012) demonstrated that when there are 'hidden profiles' in groups (that is, when members do not share all of their knowledge), the group is eight times less likely to arrive at the correct decision! Therefore, FPL managers, here is my advice to avoid the common knowledge effect:

1. Share any information which may or may not be relevant! Do not be afraid to stand out, or to be a 'maverick' – it may be that your information is vitally important to helping the community avoid making a devastating mass decision!

2. Explore different types of methods of analysis. Use multiple websites, look for new and exciting ways to analyse the statistics – any new and 'hidden' knowledge that can be delivered to the community will help to avoid the common knowledge effect.

Chapter 3:
The fear of missing out

What is FoMO?

Fear of missing out, abbreviated to **FoMO**, closely links to the previous chapter in that it can be brought on and intensified by social media interactions. FoMO is the psychological term for the "pervasive apprehension that others might have rewarding experiences from which one is absent" (Przybylski, Murayama, DeHaan & Gladwell, 2013). It is characterised by the "desire to stay continually connected with what others are doing" (Przybylski et al., 2013, p. 1843). In other words, we obsess and worry about the possibility that others may be enjoying themselves and succeeding to a greater extent than we are. As a result, we feel as though we must stay up-to-date with their every move in case they manage to do something we had not considered.

A study by JWTIntelligence (2012) found that nearly 70% of adults admit to experiencing feelings of 'missing out' (as cited in, Abel, Buff, & Burr, 2016). Further, males were more likely than females to become obsessive with social media when experiencing FoMO. Since there is undoubtedly a larger percentage of males playing FPL and on social media platforms discussing FPL, this is a worrying finding.

For those with a tendency to experience FoMO, social media can be a dangerous catalyst. The advancement of social media has made receiving information relating to FPL more accessible than ever before and, as such, the fear of missing out and the desire to stay connected to everyone's moves has become that of an addiction – "what happens if the Twitter community have made a transfer/captaincy decision that I have not considered and as a result all of the Twitter community will be successful and happy while I might not?" Or, "what happens if the community are discussing a new £4.0m defender that is guaranteed to start this gameweek and I don't check Twitter, missing out on the chance to have their points?" Not only this, but the speed of FPL on social media (especially Twitter) is unbelievably fast and ever-changing. One day away from Twitter and you can miss an abundance of information that may have been able to aid your decision-making for the upcoming gameweek. The potential to miss out on rewarding experiences and useful information amplifies FoMO and arguably excuses the desire to stay constantly connected.

Questionnaire 1 – Are you prone to FoMO?

To help us decipher whether you are someone that may be prone to experiencing FoMO, I will be asking you to complete the **self-report questionnaire** below. A self-report questionnaire in psychology is a form of survey, poll, or questionnaire in which the individual is asked to read the question and provide an answer themselves without interference from the researcher. This is one of four self-report questionnaires located throughout the book, and they are aimed at providing you with insight as to your decision-making and FPL management style.

Each questionnaire will follow the same format. The questionnaire will be introduced, instructions provided, the questionnaire will then be presented, and finally instructions will be given on how to score the questionnaire. Once you have your score, we will discuss what this can tell you about your cognitions, decision-making or behaviour, and how this may influence FPL.

Instructions

The table contains a collection of statements about your everyday experiences. Using the scale provided, please indicate how true each statement is of your general experiences by circling the appropriate response. Please answer according to what really reflects your experiences rather than what you think your experiences should be. Please treat each item separately from every other item.

This questionnaire has been taken from Przybylski et al. (2013) and moderately adapted for use in this book. For more information, please see their paper in the references section.

	Definitely **not** true of myself	**Not** true of myself	Neither true nor untrue	True of myself	Definitely true of myself
1. I fear others may have more rewarding experiences than me	1	2	3	4	5
	Definitely **not** true of myself	**Not** true of myself	Neither true nor untrue	True of myself	Definitely true of myself
2. I fear my friends may have more rewarding experiences than me	1	2	3	4	5
	Definitely **not** true of myself	**Not** true of myself	Neither true nor untrue	True of myself	Definitely true of myself
3. I get worried when I find out my friends are having fun without me	1	2	3	4	5
	Definitely **not** true of myself	**Not** true of myself	Neither true nor untrue	True of myself	Definitely true of myself
4. I get anxious when I don't know what my friends are up to	1	2	3	4	5
	Definitely **not** true of myself	**Not** true of myself	Neither true nor untrue	True of myself	Definitely true of myself
5. It is important that I understand my friends' 'in jokes'	1	2	3	4	5

	Definitely **not** true of myself	**Not** true of myself	Neither true nor untrue	True of myself	Definitely true of myself
6. Sometimes, I wonder if I spend too much time keeping up with what is going on	1	2	3	4	5
	Definitely **not** true of myself	**Not** true of myself	Neither true nor untrue	True of myself	Definitely true of myself
7. It bothers me when I miss an opportunity to meet up with friends	1	2	3	4	5
	Definitely **not** true of myself	**Not** true of myself	Neither true nor untrue	True of myself	Definitely true of myself
8. When I have a good time it is important for me to share the details online (e.g., updating status, tweeting)	1	2	3	4	5
	Definitely **not** true of myself	**Not** true of myself	Neither true nor untrue	True of myself	Definitely true of myself
9. When I miss out on a planned get-together it bothers me	1	2	3	4	5
	Definitely **not** true of myself	**Not** true of myself	Neither true nor untrue	True of myself	Definitely true of myself
10. When I go on vacation, I continue to keep tabs on what my friends are doing	1	2	3	4	5

Scoring and interpreting the questionnaire

This questionnaire has 10 questions. For each question you will have circled a score ranging from 1 to 5. Your first task is to add up all of the points, and write the total in the box below. For example, if you circled 2 for all of the statements, your total score would be 20. Total scores can range from 10 to 50, therefore your total score should fall in that range. See the box below for a visual breakdown of the various scoring categories.

/50

10-17	18-25	26-34	35-42	43-50
Very low FoMO propensity	Low FoMO propensity	Intermediate FoMO propensity	High FoMO Propensity	Very high FoMO Propensity

You should now have a better idea of the type of person you are with respect to your general FoMO propensity.

You can complete this section by filling in the below sentence:

I have _____ propensity to experience FoMO.

Why does FoMO occur?

Now we know what it is, we will briefly explore the psychology underpinning FoMO. At a basic level, FoMO can be explained through **self-determination theory** (SDT; Deci & Ryan, 1985). This theory posits that effective self-regulation and psychological health are met through the satisfaction of three basic psychological needs: competence (the ability to effectively and successfully act/behave in the world); autonomy (the ability to act independently and by choice); and relatedness (to be close and connected to others) (Przybylski et al., 2013). Therefore, for humans to be satisfied in life, we must feel that we have the ability to control our behaviours, feel as though we have free-will and choice, and feel connected to other people. Specifically, the desire to be competent and the desire to be related are potentially what drives FoMO in FPL. We want to feel (and appear) competent in our decision-making and we also want to constantly stay connected to other FPL accounts. As a result, our desire to be competent and successful will naturally be heavily influenced by the accounts we are connected to.

To explain this as a thought process:

"I want to be the best FPL player on Twitter and succeed this season"

"I am seeing other FPL managers make XYZ decisions,
what if I don't make those choices and as a result I drop in rank
and look incompetent?"

"I must make the same decisions as them in order to avoid missing out"

This right here is FoMO at its finest and closely correlates to groupthink and herd mentality.

How does FoMO affect our functioning and well-being?

We now know what FoMO is, our own propensity for it and some of the psychology underpinning it. But what are the potential consequences of it? Turkle (2011) explains that FoMO can degrade our wellbeing and cause us to have a 'tethered **sense of self**' as we are constantly second-guessing our decisions. Furthermore, being constantly active on social media can distract us from social experiences in the here-and-now (Przybylski et al., 2013), resulting in further social isolation and becoming disillusioned with the social media bubble we previously discussed.

Wortham (2011) supports this claim, emphasising that FoMO could be a primary source of negative mood because it undermines our feelings of contentment with our decisions (Przybylski et al., 2013). In other words, constantly staying connected to other people's decisions makes us question our own decisions and behaviours, leading to a fragmented sense of self. At the very worst, this could cause an **identity crisis**.

Therefore, we must try to self-regulate our FoMO and acknowledge that our decisions are worthwhile and, ultimately, the most important ones we should consider.

Applying our knowledge of FoMO to FPL

Now that we understand some of the basic psychology behind FoMO and what it could potentially mean for our sense of happiness and wellbeing, what does this mean in relation to FPL? What should you do? Or more accurately, what should you *not* do?

I believe that manoeuvring FPL is all about the attitude you take to decision-making and, most importantly, to incorrect decisions. The list I am about to give of things to avoid are only relevant if you believe that you are prone to negative mood when experiencing FoMO and if you feel anxiety if you are missing out on a player, captaincy decision or transfer. With a positive mindset, FoMO as a moderate state of mind can be an adaptive tendency which allows us to remain in touch with our friends and the community. It is also important to note that FoMO does not necessarily lead to the incorrect decision being made. Instead, FoMO influences how we weigh up our options and, as such, can heavily bias our decisions. However, as a general rule of thumb, here are some examples of things to avoid that are associated with FoMO:

1. Do not chase points due to FoMO. If a player fits your team budget and YOU want to transfer them in without a massive change to your structure, then by all means do – that is a sensible decision. However, do not transfer someone in just because they returned in the last two games and you are 'fearful' that they will continue to rise in price, continue to punish you and leave you missing out on the fun.

2. Avoid the captaincy bandwagons. By following bandwagons, the source of your decision is external (not coming from your own research or intuition). If the result is a negative one, you may be left resenting your fellow managers. Try to avoid taking into account ownership and mass decisions when captaining a player.

3. Stop changing your Goalkeeper (GK). The biggest FoMO often comes from GKs with good form. Due to the possibility of save points and bonus points, often a couple of consecutive clean sheets for a highly owned GK can be a disaster for your rank (I am looking at you Nick Pope and Emi Martinez!). However, by the time you change your GK to the one with 2-3 consecutive clean sheets, it is just as plausible that your original GK goes on a nice run himself! Set-and-forget; it is key.

4. Remember that you cannot own everyone. It is not feasible to own every popular player in the game, due to both budget and formational constraints. Remember that there are multiple avenues for points and even if there is a player scoring points in the last few weeks, you can easily choose another player that could match him. When you make peace with this idea of not being able to own everyone, it will make it a lot easier for you to avoid FoMO.

Chapter 4:
Conducting your own FPL research

Creating a narrative that does not exist

As well as digesting the content created by the community, as FPL managers we like to collect our own data to drive our own decisions, whether it be xG and xA (expected goals and expected assists), shots in the box, or key chances created per 90. However, even while collecting objective data, we are prone to applying our cognitive biases. In particular, especially as romantic football fans, we enjoy building narratives around games, players, and performances.

"Harry Kane always scores against Leicester."

"Bruno Fernandes can only perform away from Old Trafford."

"Mohamed Salah does not blank in consecutive home games."

These are just three of the narratives that I saw heavily touted at the beginning of the 2020/21 season, shortly before all three were proven incorrect on some level. Indeed, while Harry Kane's record against Leicester is fantastic and that might give him a slight boost in confidence, it is very difficult to justify "Kane always scores against Leicester" as a reason to captain him. Leicester have had six managers in the last six years, as well as hundreds of variations of players and play styles. As such, the 'Leicester' that Kane always scores against, is a very different outfit on each occasion. This general tendency to create a narrative that does not exist is known as **narrative bias**. Simply put, narrative bias is the tendency for humans to make sense of the world through stories. Due to the sheer amount of information we process on a daily basis, we often unintentionally mould incoming information around a set of narratives and ignore or refute information which does not fit the pre-existing narrative that we have built.

While narrative bias can help to explain our general tendency to manipulate information to suit a narrative, there is a well known fallacy that we engage in which may help to explain the narrative bias. Here, I am referring to the **correlation-causation fallacy**. The correlation-causation fallacy (often termed 'correlation does not imply causation') is the tendency to mistakenly assume a cause-and-effect relationship between two variables, when there is in fact only a correlation between them. A very simple demonstration of this is the following:

"Every time I go to sleep the sun rises in the morning. Therefore, my going to sleep causes the sun to rise."

While it is indeed true that these two events (sleeping and the sun rising) often coincide, it does not mean that your sleeping is causing the sun to rise, but instead that they often both occur at a similar time. This concept of inaccurately assuming causation can apply very well to FPL.

An example of the correlation-causation fallacy from the 2020/21 season was the form of Jack Grealish in the first half of the campaign. A small group of individuals began to notice that every three games, Jack Grealish delivered a double-digit haul (10+ FPL points). In fact, this pattern appeared to repeat itself four times in a row (see image). As such, if Grealish blanked twice in a row, some managers were scared to sell him as the data demonstrated that he hauled every three games.

GW	OPP	Pts	MP
2	SHU (H) 1 - 0	3	90
3	FUL (A) 0 - 3	8	90
4	LIV (H) 7 - 2	24	90
5	LEI (A) 0 - 1	3	90
6	LEE (H) 0 - 3	1	90
7	SOU (H) 3 - 4	15	90
8	ARS (A) 0 - 3	6	90
9	BHA (H) 1 - 2	1	90
10	WHU (A) 2 - 1	10	90
12	WOL (A) 0 - 1	2	90
13	BUR (H) 0 - 0	3	90
14	WBA (A) 0 - 3	10	90

This is, of course, an example of the correlation-causation fallacy. While there is no denying that there is a correlation between his best performances and how often these occur, this does not mean that his performances are caused by the fact that it is his third game. Each opponent is different and each match will play out in a different way. Therefore, be very careful assuming that simply because two events or variables coincide, one must be causing the other.

Finally, there are more specific biases relating to collection of objective data (e.g., trends over the past few gameweeks). That being, the **clustering illusion** and **phantom patterns**. The clustering illusion is a cognitive bias that often goes under the radar, but is particularly applicable to FPL. It is the tendency to mistakenly consider the inevitable 'streaks' or 'clusters' arising in small samples from random distributions to be non-random. In other words, we try to attribute meaning to random and unrelated events in small samples, causing us to see phantom patterns. This is a form of **apophenia** – the tendency to mistakenly perceive connections and meaning between unrelated things. In FPL, this can often happen, where we spot random small streaks of data and attribute meaning to them in an attempt to provide a reason to bring a specific player into our teams.

It is worth noting that often there will be meaningful data arising from small streaks or clusters. However, the issue arises when we push ourselves to look for these and persevere until we find some statistics that support the decision we wish to make. If you are finding yourself actively looking for some data to support your prior belief (confirmation bias), it is likely you will eventually stumble across the clustering illusion.

My advice to help avoid the clustering illusion is as follows:

1. Seek information from a variety of sources – it may be that once you consider the information in a different context, or in a different visual form, that you realise it has created the appearance of a 'streak' or 'spike', but that it is indeed, an illusion.

2. Increase the sample size to more than just one or two gameweeks – do not just look at statistics from the past one or two gameweeks when looking to bring a player in. Explore statistics from the previous 3-5 gameweeks and then compare this to the season-long data, as this is the best way to accurately identify a trend or correlation (another caveat

here, in that upside chasing and attacking strategies in FPL may require being reactive to single gameweek statistics and subtle trends in data).

The framing effect

The second cognitive bias we should be aware of when completing FPL research is the **framing effect,** which is similar in essence to confirmation bias. The framing effect is the tendency for our decision-making to be dependent on how the set of options or data is presented or interpreted (Gonzalez, Dana, Koshino & Just, 2005). The usual comparison in framing is positive versus negative. Here is an example of a scenario in FPL which could be framed both positively and negatively:

Framing effect in FPL	
Scenario	
Jamie Vardy has scored 14 goals from 50 shots, with five of the 14 goals from penalties.	
Positive Frame	**Negative Frame**
Jamie Vardy has scored 28% of shots he has taken this season in the Premier League. That means he is scoring almost 1 in 3 of his attempts on goal! He is also on penalties, which makes him even more of a goal-threat.	Jamie Vardy is failing to score 72% of his attempts on goal this season in the Premier League. That means he is failing to score approximately 3 out of every 4 shots. Also, 5 of his goals scored were penalties, which means that his conversion rate is probably even worse if you take away those!

Here you can see the same objective data of scoring 14 goals from 50 shots being interpreted in two very different ways, simply by framing the information in a different manner. This demonstrates that we can apply our own subjective cognitive biases when we interpret information, depending on whether we have an underlying preference. My primary piece of advice when looking at objective data is to take a step back and consider whether you are framing the data in a fashion which could be positively or negatively skewing the raw values. To take this further, you can write down how the data could be positively, and negatively, framed. Once you have done this, you will hopefully be able to see how framing the information has distorted the objective, raw values.

The law of instrument bias

The final cognitive bias that we must look out for when conducting our FPL research is the **law of instrument bias**. This is a cognitive bias involving an over-reliance on a familiar tool. In FPL, this may be the over-reliance on one specific website, or perhaps one specific type of statistic (e.g., expected stats). The law of instrument bias is generally attributed to Maslow (1966), with his famous quote:

> *"I suppose it is tempting, if the only tool you have is a hammer, to treat everything as if it were a nail."*

If you always use the same method for approaching data analysis and research, you will often miss other key pieces of data that may aid your decision-making. For example, key chances created is a great statistic for deciding whether or not to bring in a creative midfielder. However, a pass is only counted as a key chance created if the player on the other end of the pass makes contact with the football. Therefore, if Kevin de Bruyne makes a 50-yard diagonal pass onto Sterling's foot from 6 yards out but Sterling misses the ball, the statistics will not count this as a key chance. Therefore, the eye test would probably aid the statistics in this scenario.

Overall, my advice for this section is to always be open-minded when researching and always be willing to consider new ways of analysing information.

Chapter 5: Rejecting new information – closed-mindedness

As human beings, and even more so as FPL managers, we can often be quite stubborn. While it may appear that this is always deliberate, our cognitive biases can cause us to be stubborn without our conscious knowledge. This is possibly one of the more interesting sub-groups of cognitive biases and one of my personal favourites.

Conservatism bias

The most commonly talked about bias in this area is **conservatism bias**. Most often discussed in the world of behavioural finance, conservatism bias is the tendency to insufficiently revise one's belief when presented with new information. This can lead to the individual failing to react to the presentation of new information in a rational manner (Pompian, 2012). This mental process is especially detrimental in the world of finance, but can also be detrimental in the world of FPL. For example, an inability to respond to new information can lead to managers missing out on big points hauls, keeping specific players too long, or missing out on price rises.

Semmelweis reflex

Very closely linked to conservatism bias is the **Semmelweis reflex**. The Semmelweis reflex is the tendency to reject new information that contradicts our already established beliefs and ideas (Gupta, Saini, Oberoi, Kalra, & Nasir, 2020). The term originates from 1847, when Hungarian physician Ignaz Semmelweis discovered (20 years before Germ Theory was discovered) that washing hands after performing autopsies and between patients, reduced childbed fever mortality rates ten-fold.

However, most of the physicians rejected this empirical evidence as it did not conform to their prior beliefs, such as the belief that a gentleman's hands could not transmit disease. It is easier to reject evidence that does not fit our prior beliefs than to update and restructure our existing belief system.

The key difference between conservatism bias and the Semmelweis reflex, is that conservatism bias is the inability to update our beliefs, whereas Semmelweis reflex is reflective of the direct rejection of new information due to its contradiction with our already established cognitions and beliefs. Therefore, the Semmelweis reflex is more explicit and deliberate than conservatism bias. However, they both represent a very similar concept, in that we can often be closed-minded when presented with new information.

Plan continuation bias

Lastly on this topic is one of my personal favourites to discuss in relation to FPL – the **plan continuation bias**. I regularly experience this cognitive bias and it is, therefore, the one that I often try to remind myself of on a weekly basis.

The plan continuation bias is the tendency for an individual to continue with the original plan, despite this plan no longer being viable, or better alternatives since arising. A good example of this in FPL is the transferring in of specific players for a set number of gameweeks.

Hypothetical example:

"I am going 'big at the back' this season as the premium full-backs offer lots of potential going forward and their fixtures are good for the first six gameweeks."

However, after two gameweeks, all of the attacking full-backs are struggling with attacking returns and clean sheets, and many of the equally-priced attackers are scoring for fun. Suffering from the plan continuation bias, you may continue with the premium defenders as that was the original plan. However, being adaptive in FPL is vital and, therefore, at least considering altering your original plan here would be advised.

It is worth noting that there is a fine line between plan continuation bias and correctly refraining from being short-sighted and over-reactive. It is up to us as FPL managers to decide when we are merely being patient and trusting the process, or failing to react and adapt to a dynamic and ever-changing game.

P◆RT TWO

MAKING YOUR
FPL DECISIONS

Introduction to Part Two

After the drawn-out pre-gameweek stage, it is finally time to make your decisions. These decisions are normally made on the Thursday or Friday prior to the Friday evening or Saturday morning deadline, but can be made throughout the week as well. Often these decisions are the result of your week of preparation, or sometimes they are in response to the press conferences.

Either way, there are multiple concepts and biases to consider when we make decisions. As we move toward the actual decision-making processes of humans, we will delve deeper into the field of cognitive psychology.

Chapter 6:
Gut feeling – can we trust it?

An introduction to gut feeling

We begin Part 2 with a very important and widely discussed area of FPL decision-making – whether or not we should trust our gut feeling. How many times has someone told you to "go with your gut" or "trust your instinct"? Or, how many times have you thought to yourself, "I should have just trusted my gut"? These are some common phrases that are bandied around, but do they hold any weight? Is gut feeling a reliable tool to aid your decisions, or will it likely lead you astray?

Since the dawn of man, emotions have been the primary tool used to aid and drive decision-making as they tell you various details about the decision to be made. For example, if you are approached by a lion you may have the emotion of fear, which informs you to be careful in this situation. Damasio (1994) argues that emotion is a cognitive process that contributes to logical thinking and, therefore, we should be careful not to disregard our emotional responses. Often, these emotions can combine with past experiences (failures and successes) to create what we refer to as a 'gut feeling'.

The best definition for gut feeling is an immediate reaction, feeling or preference, without conscious reasoning or analysis. A **gut feeling** can also be described as a 'deep knowing', **'intuition'** or a 'hunch'. Throughout this chapter and the remainder of the book, 'gut feeling' and 'intuition' will be used interchangeably to reflect the same concept.

Research over the past 15 years has focused on decision-making in reference to two systems of thinking: the 'analytic/rational system' and the 'experiential system' (Gutnik, Forogh Hakimzada, Yoskowitz, & Patel, 2006, as cited in, Soosalu, Henwood, & Deo, 2019). This was extended and popularised by Daniel Kahneman, who split reasoning and decision-making into two systems (Kahneman, 2011).

System 1 thinking is fast, intuitive and reliant on emotional input (namely, gut feeling). **System 2 thinking** is slower, driven by logic and reasoning, and analytical by nature (rational thinking). The question, therefore, is how much weight should we give to our System 1 thinking? In 50-50 decisions in FPL, should we let our System 1 thinking dominate, or rely on statistics, logic and deliberate reasoning driven by our System 2 thinking? Before considering the advantages and disadvantages of intuition and rational thinking, it is important to explore whether you are a naturally intuitive or rational individual, which will be achieved through completion of the second questionnaire in this book.

Questionnaire 2 – Are you intuitive or rational?

Instructions

Using the following scale, please rate the extent to which you believe these statements reflect your thinking and behaviour (by circling the relevant response), ranging from definitely not true of myself to definitely true of myself. Please consider each question separately from the rest. For ease of understanding, the 40-item questionnaire has been split into two parts, each with 20 questions. At the end, there are instructions on how to score and evaluate your answers. Good luck!

This questionnaire has been taken from Keaton (2017) and Pacini and Epstein (1999), moderately adapted for use in this book. In particular, the items have been randomised and adapted to only require one form of coding. For more information, please see their papers in the References section.

	Definitely **not** true of myself	**Not** true of myself	Neither true nor untrue	True of myself	Definitely true of myself
1. I am good at figuring out complicated problems	1	2	3	4	5
	Definitely **not** true of myself	**Not** true of myself	Neither true nor untrue	True of myself	Definitely true of myself
2. I am good at solving problems that require careful logical analysis	1	2	3	4	5
	Definitely **not** true of myself	**Not** true of myself	Neither true nor untrue	True of myself	Definitely true of myself
3. I am a very analytical thinker	1	2	3	4	5
	Definitely **not** true of myself	**Not** true of myself	Neither true nor untrue	True of myself	Definitely true of myself
4. Reasoning things out carefully is one of my strong points	1	2	3	4	5
	Definitely **not** true of myself	**Not** true of myself	Neither true nor untrue	True of myself	Definitely true of myself
5. I reason well under pressure	1	2	3	4	5
	Definitely **not** true of myself	**Not** true of myself	Neither true nor untrue	True of myself	Definitely true of myself
6. I am much better at figuring things out logically than most people	1	2	3	4	5

	Definitely not true of myself	Not true of myself	Neither true nor untrue	True of myself	Definitely true of myself
7. I have a logical mind	1	2	3	4	5
	Definitely not true of myself	Not true of myself	Neither true nor untrue	True of myself	Definitely true of myself
8. I have no problem thinking things through carefully	1	2	3	4	5
	Definitely not true of myself	Not true of myself	Neither true nor untrue	True of myself	Definitely true of myself
9. Using logic usually works well for me in figuring out problems in my life	1	2	3	4	5
	Definitely not true of myself	Not true of myself	Neither true nor untrue	True of myself	Definitely true of myself
10. I usually have clear, explainable reasons for my decisions	1	2	3	4	5
	Definitely not true of myself	Not true of myself	Neither true nor untrue	True of myself	Definitely true of myself
11. I don't avoid situations that require thinking in depth about something	1	2	3	4	5
	Definitely not true of myself	Not true of myself	Neither true nor untrue	True of myself	Definitely true of myself
12. I enjoy intellectual challenges	1	2	3	4	5

	Definitely not true of myself	Not true of myself	Neither true nor untrue	True of myself	Definitely true of myself
13. I like to have to do a lot of thinking	1	2	3	4	5
	Definitely not true of myself	Not true of myself	Neither true nor untrue	True of myself	Definitely true of myself
14. I enjoy solving problems that require hard thinking	1	2	3	4	5
	Definitely not true of myself	Not true of myself	Neither true nor untrue	True of myself	Definitely true of myself
15. Thinking is my idea of an enjoyable activity	1	2	3	4	5
	Definitely not true of myself	Not true of myself	Neither true nor untrue	True of myself	Definitely true of myself
16. I prefer complex problems to simple problems	1	2	3	4	5
	Definitely not true of myself	Not true of myself	Neither true nor untrue	True of myself	Definitely true of myself
17. Thinking hard and for a long time about something gives me satisfaction	1	2	3	4	5
	Definitely not true of myself	Not true of myself	Neither true nor untrue	True of myself	Definitely true of myself
18. I enjoy thinking in abstract terms	1	2	3	4	5

	Definitely not true of myself	Not true of myself	Neither true nor untrue	True of myself	Definitely true of myself
19. Knowing the answer without having to understand the reasoning behind it is not good enough for me	1	2	3	4	5
	Definitely not true of myself	Not true of myself	Neither true nor untrue	True of myself	Definitely true of myself
20. Learning new ways to think would be very appealing to me	1	2	3	4	5

Scoring and interpreting part one of this questionnaire

The first 20 questions of this questionnaire measure your ability and your tendency to use logic when making decisions (i.e., rational thinking). In other words, do you have the ability/pre-disposition to think logically, and do you usually use logic when executing your decisions? Add up the score for each of the 20 questions to get your total. Your score can range from 20-100, with 20 reflecting an absence of rational thinking, and a score of 100 reflecting high rational thinking.

/100

We will now continue with part two of this questionnaire, the second 20 items.

	Definitely **not** true of myself	**Not** true of myself	Neither true nor untrue	True of myself	Definitely true of myself
21. I have very good intuition	1	2	3	4	5
	Definitely **not** true of myself	**Not** true of myself	Neither true nor untrue	True of myself	Definitely true of myself
22. Using my gut feelings usually works well for me in figuring out problems in my life	1	2	3	4	5
	Definitely **not** true of myself	**Not** true of myself	Neither true nor untrue	True of myself	Definitely true of myself
23. I believe in trusting my hunches	1	2	3	4	5
	Definitely **not** true of myself	**Not** true of myself	Neither true nor untrue	True of myself	Definitely true of myself
24. I trust my initial feelings about people	1	2	3	4	5
	Definitely **not** true of myself	**Not** true of myself	Neither true nor untrue	True of myself	Definitely true of myself
25. When it comes to trusting people, I can usually rely on my gut feeling	1	2	3	4	5
	Definitely **not** true of myself	**Not** true of myself	Neither true nor untrue	True of myself	Definitely true of myself
26. If I were to rely on my gut feeling, I would rarely make mistakes	1	2	3	4	5

	Definitely not true of myself	Not true of myself	Neither true nor untrue	True of myself	Definitely true of myself
27. I hardly ever go wrong when I listen to my deepest gut feeling to find an answer	1	2	3	4	5
	Definitely not true of myself	Not true of myself	Neither true nor untrue	True of myself	Definitely true of myself
28. My snap judgements are probably better than most people's	1	2	3	4	5
	Definitely not true of myself	Not true of myself	Neither true nor untrue	True of myself	Definitely true of myself
29. I can usually feel when a person is right or wrong, even if I cannot explain how I know	1	2	3	4	5
	Definitely not true of myself	Not true of myself	Neither true nor untrue	True of myself	Definitely true of myself
30. I suspect my hunches are accurate more often than not	1	2	3	4	5
	Definitely not true of myself	Not true of myself	Neither true nor untrue	True of myself	Definitely true of myself
31. I like to rely on my intuitive impressions	1	2	3	4	5
	Definitely not true of myself	Not true of myself	Neither true nor untrue	True of myself	Definitely true of myself
32. Intuition can be a very useful way to solve problems	1	2	3	4	5

	Definitely not true of myself	Not true of myself	Neither true nor untrue	True of myself	Definitely true of myself
33. I often go by my instincts when deciding on a course of action	1	2	3	4	5

	Definitely not true of myself	Not true of myself	Neither true nor untrue	True of myself	Definitely true of myself
34. I enjoy situations in which I have to rely on intuition	1	2	3	4	5

	Definitely not true of myself	Not true of myself	Neither true nor untrue	True of myself	Definitely true of myself
35. I think there ae times when one should rely on one's intuition	1	2	3	4	5

	Definitely not true of myself	Not true of myself	Neither true nor untrue	True of myself	Definitely true of myself
36. I think it is wise to make important decisions based on feelings	1	2	3	4	5

	Definitely not true of myself	Not true of myself	Neither true nor untrue	True of myself	Definitely true of myself
37. I think it is a good idea to rely on one's intuition for important decisions	1	2	3	4	5

	Definitely not true of myself	Not true of myself	Neither true nor untrue	True of myself	Definitely true of myself
38. I generally depend on my feelings to help me make decisions	1	2	3	4	5

	Definitely not true of myself	Not true of myself	Neither true nor untrue	True of myself	Definitely true of myself
39. I would happily depend on an individual that described himself or herself as intuitive	1	2	3	4	5
	Definitely not true of myself	Not true of myself	Neither true nor untrue	True of myself	Definitely true of myself
40. I tend to use my heart as a guide for my actions	1	2	3	4	5

Scoring and interpreting part two of this questionnaire

The second 20 questions of this questionnaire measure your ability and your tendency to use gut feeling when making decisions. In other words, do you have the ability/pre-disposition to think intuitively (use your gut feeling), and do you usually use intuition when executing your decisions? Add up the score for each of the 20 questions to get your total. Your score can range from 20-100, with 20 reflecting an absence of gut feeling in your decision-making, and a score of 100 reflecting high use of gut feeling in your decision-making.

/100

Bringing the two parts together – summary of scores

Rational Score (Logic)	Intuitive Score (Gut Feeling)
/100	/100

While there is no official cut off to suggest what is 'high' or 'low', I would suggest that anything below 50 could be considered on the low side, and anything above 70 could be considered on the high side. You can complete this section by filling in the below sentence:

I am a(n) _____ individual, and therefore I should

make my decisions based on _____.

Understanding how trusting your gut feeling impacts FPL

In the table below, you can see the differences between the intuitive (gut feeling) and rational (logic) systems. Having totalled your scores, consider the characteristics that reflect both your score and who you are as a person.

Comparison of the intuitive and rational systems	
Intuitive System (Gut Feeling)	Rational System (Logic)
Holistic	Analytic
Automatic, effortless	Intentional, effortful
Affective: pleasure-pain oriented (what feels good)	Logical: reason oriented (what is rational)
Associationistic connections (making mental connections between feelings or events)	Logical connections
Behaviour mediated by "vibes" from past events	Behaviour mediated by conscious appraisal of events
Encodes reality in concrete images, metaphors and narratives	Encodes reality in abstract symbols, words and numbers
More rapid processing: oriented toward immediate action	Slower processing: oriented toward delayed action
Slower and more resistant to change: change with repetitive or intense experience	Changes more rapidly and easily: changes with strength or argument and new evidence
More crudely differentiated: broad generalisation gradient; stereotypical thinking	More highly differentiated
More crudely integrated: dissociative, emotional complexes; context-specific processing	More highly integrated: context-general principles
Experienced passively and preconsciously: we are seized by our emotions	Experienced actively and consciously: we are in control of our thoughts
Self-evidently valid: "experiencing is believing"	Requires justification via logic and evidence

Epstein (1991, as cited in, Epstein, Pacini, Denes-Raj, & Heier, 1996).
The previous table on the rational and intuitive systems has been taken
from Epstein et al. (1996, p. 391) and moderately adapted for use in this
book. Full credit for this material goes to the team of authors. See the
original and full paper in the References section.

Evidence in favour of using gut feeling

After introducing you to gut feeling and finding out just how much
you trust your intuition, it is worth exploring whether it is a positive
or negative attribute – should we trust our intuition? The first piece of
evidence to suggest that gut feeling is more than just a combination of
emotional impulses, is discussed by Sadler-Smith and Shefy (2004).
The authors explain that there is an increasing cohort of literature
highlighting how much of cognition can occur automatically outside of
consciousness and in the realm of intuition. In other words, many of the
complex thought processes and connections that we make occur outside of
our conscious knowledge. Therefore, intuition could in fact be the result
of automatic, complex thought processes that are simply too fast for us to
process consciously, resulting in the impression of a 'hunch'.

Furthermore, there is a school of thought which suggests that gut feeling
could be the synthesis of diverse experiences, all brought together into an
integrated picture (Khatri & Ng, 2000). In other words, we automatically
(without conscious processing) connect all of our past failures and
successes, allowing us to understand how our new decision relates to our
past experiences. If this is indeed true, gut feeling and FPL pair together
fantastically well, as our gut feeling can pull on past experiences where we
have failed and succeeded and compile them together.

Imagine a scenario whereby you are trying to decide whether or not to play
your Wildcard chip in gameweek 3, or wait and play the chip in a later
gameweek (see Chapter 16). In this scenario, your gut feeling is telling you
that it is not the best time to play the chip, even though other managers are
playing it and you accept there are some benefits to it. Your gut feeling is
telling you to wait. The above research suggests that rather than it being
guesswork, your gut feeling could actually be the result of connections
and decisions being made outside of your conscious knowledge, combining
your experience from previous years of playing and advising the optimal

path for you at that point. Whether or not this is true is hard to know, but it would still be wise to at least consider what your gut is telling you!

Looking more specifically at how gut feeling can benefit us, Khatri and Ng (2000) explain that gut feeling is best utilised in unstable situations (i.e., where the decision-making process and outcomes are constantly changing), and less so in stable situations. Due to the predictability of stable environments, utilising data and facts will often be more useful in correctly predicting the outcome than gut feeling. However, unstable environments (such as FPL) provide us with three challenges: a) time constraints; b) the need to collect and process a large amount of input and data; c) lack of consistency and reliability in the data (Khatri & Ng, 2000). In these cases, using just data and logic alone can lead to important details being missed. Further, in these situations, gut feeling can be used to pull on past experiences in order to identify which pieces of information are more important than others when making the decision. Therefore, according to this research, FPL is probably a situation whereby gut feeling could be beneficial for making decisions.

Evidence against using gut feeling

I will concede at this stage that I am a big advocate of trusting your gut feeling, mainly due to emotional reasons that we will discuss in the final section. However, there is a small cohort of research which suggests that trusting your gut feeling can result in some negative outcomes, and therefore it is important to review this research. Firstly, trusting our gut too much can engage the previously mentioned 'Semmelweis reflex', whereby we reject new information because it contradicts an already established belief or preference. In other words, holding our gut feeling as sacred and vitally important, may result in us rejecting new information that has been accurately produced by logical, data-driven reasoning.

There is also evidence that trusting your gut to a very high extent can result in 'severe and systematic errors' (Guthrie, Rachlinksi, & Wistrich, 2007). The authors demonstrated this by asking judges to complete a **cognitive reflection test,** seen in the image below (Frederick, 2005). Therefore I would like you to attempt the cognitive reflection test as well.

Cognitive reflection test

Instructions: *Answer the questions using your intuition (your gut feeling), without rational reasoning. Attempt to answer the questions within 10 seconds. Once you have noted down your gut feeling, you can then work through the questions rationally, and see if you can get the correct answers! The answers are explained after the task, but no cheating!*

1. A bat and a ball cost £1.10. The bat costs £1.00 more than the ball. How much does the ball cost?

   _____ pence

2. If it takes 5 machines 5 minutes to make 5 widgets, how long would it take 100 machines to make 100 widgets?

   _____ minutes

3. In a lake, there is a patch of lily pads. Every day, the patch doubles in size. If it takes 48 days for the patch to cover the entire lake, how long would it take for the patch to cover half of the lake?

   _____ days

THE FOLLOWING PARAGRAPHS CONTAIN THE ANSWERS TO THE ABOVE – STOP READING IF YOU ARE YET TO ATTEMPT IT.

For question 1, the answer that intuitively comes to mind is usually £0.10, or 10 pence. However, even a small amount of logical reflection will demonstrate that this is incorrect. If the ball costs 10p, and the bat is £1 more, the total would be £1.20. In fact, the correct answer here is therefore 5p: £1.05 + £0.05 = £1.10.

For question 2, the answer that usually intuitively comes to mind is 100 minutes. However, given the example that 5 machines take 5 minutes to make 5 widgets, this means that 1 machine takes 5 minutes to make 1 widget. Therefore, it would take only five minutes for 100 machines to make 100 widgets.

For question 3, the intuitive answer is 24 days, which is once again incorrect. After considering the question logically, the correct answer is 47 days. If the lily pads cover the entire lake on day 48, and doubles in size each day, the lake must have only been half covered the day before – hence the answer is 47 days (Guthrie et al., 2007).

This is simple yet striking example of how being impulsive and intuitive in our decisions is not always advisable, and can result in systematic errors (Guthrie et al., 2007). However, it is worth mentioning that these examples only permit when there is a serious time constraint (i.e., that of a few seconds). Therefore, if we can find a way to utilise our gut feeling, but not in an impulsive fashion, perhaps we can avoid many of these errors.

Does trusting your gut lead to higher enjoyment of FPL?

Perhaps at this stage you are not convinced by the hypothesised advantages of gut feeling with respect to more effective decision-making and you instead side with the hypothesis that trusting gut feeling can lead to severe and systematic errors. If this is the case, there is less of a debate surrounding the emotional benefits of trusting our gut feeling. Stevenson and Hicks (2016) showed that intuitive thinking has a strong positive relationship with happiness – simply, when we think intuitively, we are more satisfied. This is amplified when intuitive thinkers employ an intuitive decision style, that is, when the intuitive thinking is followed up by intuitive decisions. In other words, when we process thoughts according to our gut feeling and follow this through with decisions made according to gut feeling, we are more likely to experience happiness. As well as general happiness, there are further positives that result from trusting your gut feeling:

1. Trusting your gut feeling will allow you to begin to trust yourself and build confidence in the decisions that you make. You will begin to understand the way you think, why you think that way, the emotions that drive you. Learning to trust your emotional responses and the intuitive voice inside of your head will allow you to build a positive relationship with yourself.

2. Trusting your gut feeling will make it less likely that you feel frustration and resentment to those around you (i.e., the FPL Community). If you allow the group (herd mentality and groupthink) or allow a specific

person to heavily influence your decision-making process, you may resent them and feel frustrated that you did not follow your own gut feeling.

Therefore, even if you are not convinced about the prior research which suggests that gut feeling could be the synthesis of diverse experiences, it should at the very least improve feelings of happiness and self-confidence, and reduce feelings of resentment and frustration. It is worth attempting to listen to your gut feeling and learn when and where it can be most useful.

Conclusion on the use of gut feeling in FPL

Sadler-Smith and Shefy (2004) capture the viewpoint that I believe we should all have when considering the role of gut feeling in decision-making: "rather than being set in opposition to each other, creative intuition and rational analysis are better conceived as two parallel systems of knowing" (p. 76). In other words, rather than placing gut feeling on a pedestal as the only tool we should use to guide decision-making, we should consider it in unison with, and parallel to, logical and data-driven decision-making.

My own personal belief is that gut feeling is best utilised when data and logic have delivered a 50/50 decision, and do not particularly favour one over the other. Here, it may be that gut feeling can give you the edge over and above logic and, at the very least, will result in lower frustration and resentment if your gut decision is an unsuccessful one. The most applicable example of this is captaincy decisions, which is often between two premium players. If you have researched and evaluated using the eye test, statistics and all of the data that you utilise to make decisions and you are still unsure, I modestly advise that you trust your gut feeling.

"But I am not always sure what my gut is telling me."

A nice little trick here is to flip a coin. Let us use an example of captaining Sterling or Salah. If the coin lands on tails, you captain Salah; and if the coin lands on heads, you captain Sterling. *Flip.* The coin lands on tails and, therefore, you have to captain Salah. Right in this moment, how do you feel? If you feel a small amount of relief and happiness, it is likely that your gut feeling was telling you to pick Salah. If you feel slight concern or you want to flip again ('best of three'), your gut feeling is probably telling you to captain Sterling. In the very rare scenario that you feel no emotion when the coin lands on heads or tails, I suppose we just let the coin decide!

Chapter 7:
Risk-taking in FPL

One of the biggest elements of FPL is risk-taking. Deciding whether or not to take risks is often the part of FPL which takes up the largest amount of our time. "Should I transfer in X player, even though he is not guaranteed to start the next game? Should I take a -8 hit to bring in an explosive yet inconsistent player? Should I captain a differential player this week, even though everyone will be captaining another player?" There are multiple ways to play FPL, from Pranil Sheth's 'upside chasing' (which has delivered multiple top-100 finishes), to Joshua Bull's patient strategy (which saw him crowned 2019/20 FPL champion). The key theme throughout this chapter is to play your own game, as either strategy can work successfully depending on your personality type.

An introduction to risk-taking

The word 'risk' refers to "situations in which a decision is made whose consequences depend on the outcomes of future events having known probabilities" (Lopes, 1987, p. 255). In other words, risk is the completion of an action in the anticipation that a future event will occur in a specific fashion. The issue is, these probabilities are not exact and, often (as is the case with FPL), the projected outcome can be largely different to the actual outcome. It is often the case that the larger the uncertainty in the outcome (the less accurately we are able to predict the outcome), the greater the risk. As such, many moves made in FPL (whereby the outcome is often largely unknown) can be considered 'risky'. It is our responsibility as managers to attempt to understand the fine line between taking risks and being foolish.

Risk seeking vs. risk averse

Building on the above definition of risk, experimental psychologists have generally gone down the route of attempting to label individuals according to two profiles: **risk seeking** or **risk averse**. On one hand, risk seeking is a term used to describe individuals who tend to accept greater uncertainty in exchange for greater rewards. Risk is normally considered attractive and necessary to these individuals. On the other hand, risk averse is a term used to describe individuals who tend to be reluctant to take risks and would rather settle for lower risk, lower reward. Risk is normally considered unfavourable and unnecessary to these individuals.

A classic method for identifying whether someone is risk averse or risk seeking is by completing Kahneman and Tversky's (1979) experimental task. You can be the participant in this case, by answering the two questions below.

Risk seeking or risk averse? (Kahneman & Tversky, 1979)
1.   Which would you rather have: £3,000 guaranteed, or an 80% chance of winning £4,000?
2.   Which would you rather have: 90% chance of winning £3,000, or a 45% chance of winning £6,000?

Despite the expected value of the gamble being higher than the guaranteed in the first question (.80 x £4,000 = £3,200), 'risk averse' individuals tend to favour the guaranteed money. Similarly, risk averse individuals will also tend to favour the 90% chance in the second question, despite it having the same expected value as the 45% chance (.90 x £3,000 = £2,700; .45 x £6,000 = £2,700) and the lower ceiling. As well as this classic task by Kahneman and Tversky (1979), we are able to ascertain our risk-taking propensity via a self-report questionnaire.

Questionnaire 3 - Are you risk seeking or risk averse?

As you will see throughout this chapter, I strongly urge you to play your own game and, therefore, having a better sense of your own risk-taking propensity will allow you to fine-tune your game to suit your personality. Therefore, the next section of this chapter brings to you the third questionnaire of this book.

Instructions

Please answer each question as honestly as possible. You can answer each item according to five responses: 'strongly disagree', 'disagree', 'neither agree nor disagree', 'agree', 'strongly agree'. If more than one answer is applicable, please choose the most applicable answer, as you cannot circle two answers. At the end, there are instructions on how to score and evaluate your answers. Good luck!

This questionnaire has been taken from Zhang, Highouse and Nye (2018) and moderately adapted for use in this book. It is known as the General Risk-Taking Propensity Scale (GRiPS). For more information, please see their paper in the references section.

	Definitely **not** true of myself	**Not** true of myself	Neither true nor untrue	True of myself	Definitely true of myself
1. Taking risks makes life more fun	1	2	3	4	5
	Definitely **not** true of myself	**Not** true of myself	Neither true nor untrue	True of myself	Definitely true of myself
2. My friends would say that I'm a risk-taker	1	2	3	4	5
	Definitely **not** true of myself	**Not** true of myself	Neither true nor untrue	True of myself	Definitely true of myself
3. I enjoy taking risks in most aspects of my life	1	2	3	4	5

	Definitely not true of myself	Not true of myself	Neither true nor untrue	True of myself	Definitely true of myself
4. I would take a risk even if it meant I might get hurt	1	2	3	4	5
	Definitely not true of myself	Not true of myself	Neither true nor untrue	True of myself	Definitely true of myself
5. Taking risks is an important part of my life	1	2	3	4	5
	Definitely not true of myself	Not true of myself	Neither true nor untrue	True of myself	Definitely true of myself
6. I commonly make risky decisions	1	2	3	4	5
	Definitely not true of myself	Not true of myself	Neither true nor untrue	True of myself	Definitely true of myself
7. I am a believer in taking chances	1	2	3	4	5
	Definitely not true of myself	Not true of myself	Neither true nor untrue	True of myself	Definitely true of myself
8. I am attracted to, rather than scared by, risk	1	2	3	4	5

Scoring and interpreting this questionnaire

This questionnaire has 8 questions, and for each question you will have circled a score ranging from 1 to 5. Your first task is to add up all of the points, and write the total in the box below. For example, if you circled 2 for all of the statements, your total score would be 16. Total scores can range from 8 to 40, therefore your total score should fall in that range.

/40

8-13	14-19	20-28	29-34	35-40
Definite risk averse	Moderate risk averse	Intermediate risk propensity	Moderate risk seeker	Definite risk seeker

You should now have a better idea of the type of person you are with respect to your general risk-taking propensity.

You can complete this section by filling in the below sentence:

I am a(n) _____ **type, and therefore I should opt to** make _____ **decisions.**

Evidence that social media could amplify risk-taking behaviour

There is a large cohort of literature which demonstrates that social influences have an effect on risk-taking behaviours. As individuals, a key factor that influences our decisions of whether to be risk averse or risk seeking in a specific context is the social comparisons we make (McCoy & Natsuaki, 2017). In other words, we decide on, and adapt, our risk-taking behaviours based on comparisons with other individuals. While there is a large cohort of literature which suggests that **peer pressure** arising from several peers increases our risk-taking behaviour, there is also evidence that the mere presence of one friend is enough to increase our desire to take risks (e.g., O'Brien, Albert, Chein & Steinberg, 2011). In other words, our friends do not even need to be directly encouraging risky behaviour; their mere presence is enough to amplify our risk-seeking behaviours.

One can imagine, therefore, that social media can recreate this environment of peer pressure and potentially amplify it. As an example, my most popular tweet this year had just over 300,000 impressions (times people saw the tweet) and 40,000 engagements (times people interacted with this tweet). If the mere presence of one friend is enough to encourage us to be more risk seeking, the watching eyes of over a quarter of a million people could be enough to make us take some incredible risks!

Play your own game: risk-taking in FPL

Firstly, it is very important to understand that everyone has their own style of playing FPL and the most important note here is that you should play your own game. If the first task, the questionnaire and your own introspection suggests that you are a risk averse individual, then taking big hits and captaining differential players should probably not be the strategy that you deploy. If you make moves based on a style of play that does not reflect your own cognitions and behaviours (e.g., engaging in risk seeking behaviour as a risk averse individual), it will likely result in confusion and ineffectiveness long-term, reducing your enjoyment of the game.

In strategy-based games, it is important to take some risks (to a degree). Assuming you want to win FPL (or at the very least do well), to beat almost 8 million other teams you need to be willing to take risks and to time those risks perfectly. However, taking risks too early or too frequently can result in being regularly punished if the safer, template route is more successful.

My advice here is that no matter what your risk-taking propensity is, you should take some risks when playing FPL. However, you should tailor this based on the type of individual you believe yourself to be (or according to the questionnaire). The more in-line your FPL decision-making is with your natural tendencies, the more effectively you will manage to navigate the season. Lastly, be aware that social media and social interactions may encourage you to take more risks than you typically would. Attempt to make your decisions as though no-one were to see them – risky or not. If this is not possible for you, perhaps consider presenting your team less on social media. You can still engage in discussions and be present in the community, but removing the 'team reveal' aspect of social media may allow you to make more sensible decisions and take less unnecessary risks.

Chapter 8:
When should we make
FPL decisions?

This is an area of great interest to me as it applies to both personal and professional life. When used correctly, knowing our optimal time to make decisions can greatly improve our decision-making in various domains. Often we consider *why* we are making decisions, the *content* of our decisions and the potential *consequences*. However, we very rarely consider the time of day (ToD) in which we make these important decisions. Do you always make important decisions at the same ToD? Do you always confirm your FPL transfers and captaincy at the same ToD? If not, do you think that this should be consistent? If you already are consistent, have you questioned whether this is indeed the optimal time to make these key decisions? In this chapter, I will cover two alternative approaches to the question of when we should make decisions in FPL and offer my advice on which school of thought is the most compelling.

Before we begin, it is important to understand the key term that will be used throughout this chapter – that is, **chronotype**. Chronotype reflects an individual's propensity to sleep at a particular time in the standard 24-hour period, which will ultimately influence the time of day in which they are most alert, energetic and productive. In other words, due to individual differences some individuals will be most alert and productive in the morning, some in the afternoon and some in the evening. Therefore, chronotype can essentially boil down to the following question: are you a morning person or an evening person? Generally speaking, **morning types** are cognitively optimal during the morning hours, while **evening types** are cognitively optimal during the evening hours. The following questionnaire should help you to find out your chronotype.

Questionnaire 4 – What is your chronotype?

Instructions

Circle the answer that best describes how you have **felt in recent weeks**. If more than one answer is applicable, please choose the most applicable answer, as you cannot circle two answers. As per the other questionnaires throughout the book, at the end there are instructions on how to score and evaluate your answers. Good luck!

This questionnaire has been taken from Horne and Östberg (1976) and moderately adapted for use in this book. It is known as the Morningness-Eveningness Questionnaire (MEQ). For more information, please see their paper in the references section.

1. Approximately what time would you get up if you were entirely free to plan your day?	
Options	Score (please circle)
05.00 - 06.29 am	5
06.30 - 07.44 am	4
07.45 - 09.44 am	3
09.45 - 10.59 am	2
11.00 - 11.59 am	1
2. Approximately what time would you go to bed if you were entirely free to plan your evening?	
Options	Score (please circle)
20.00 - 20.59 pm	5
21.00 - 22.14 pm	4
22.15 pm - 00.29 am	3
00.30 - 01.44 am	2
01.45 - 03.00 am	1
3. If you usually have to get up at a specific time in the morning, how much do you depend on an alarm clock?	
Options	Score (please circle)
Not at all dependent	4
Slightly dependent	3
Somewhat dependent	2
Very much dependent	1

4. How easy do you find it to get up in the morning (when you are not awakened unexpectedly)?	
Options	Score (please circle)
Very easy	4
Somewhat easy	3
Somewhat difficult	2
Very difficult	1

5. How alert do you feel during the first half hour after you wake up in the morning?	
Options	Score (please circle)
Very alert	4
Fairly alert	3
Slightly alert	2
Not at all alert	1

6. How hungry do you feel during the first half hour after you wake up?	
Options	Score (please circle)
Very hungry	4
Fairly hungry	3
Slightly hungry	2
Not at all hungry	1

7. During the first half hour after you wake up in the morning, how do you feel?	
Options	Score (please circle)
Very refreshed	4
Fairly refreshed	3
Fairly tired	2
Very tired	1

8. If you had no commitments the next day, what time would you go to bed compared to your usual bedtime?	
Options	Score (please circle)
Seldom or never later	4
Less than 1 hour	3
1-2 hours later	2
More than 2 hours later	1

9. You have decided to do physical exercise. A friend suggests that you do this for one hour twice a week, and the best time for him is between 07:00 - 08:00 am. Bearing in mind nothing but your own "internal clock", how do you think you would perform?	
Options	Score (please circle)
Would be in good form	4
Would be in reasonable form	3
Would find it difficult	2
Would find it very difficult	1

10. At what time of day do you feel you become tired as a result of needing sleep?	
Options	Score (please circle)
20.00 - 20.59 pm	5
21.00 - 22.14 pm	4
22.15 pm - 00.44 am	3
00.45 - 01.59 am	2
02.00 - 03.00 am	1

11. You want to be at your peak performance for a test that you know is going to be mentally exhausting and will last for two hours. You are entirely free to plan your day. Considering only your own 'internal clock', which ONE of the four testing times would you choose?	
Options	Score (please circle)
08.00 - 10.00 am	6
11.00 am - 13.00 pm	4
15.00 - 17.00 pm	2
19.00 - 21.00 pm	0

12. If you got into bed at 11:00 pm, how tired would you be?	
Options	Score (please circle)
Very tired	5
Fairly tired	3
A little tired	2
Not at all tired	0

13. For some reason, you have gone to bed several hours later than usual, but there is no need to get up at any particular time the next morning. Which ONE of the following are you most likely to do?

Options	Score (please circle)
Will wake up at usual time, but will NOT fall back asleep	4
Will wake up at usual time and will doze thereafter	3
Will wake up at usual time but will fall asleep again	2
Will NOT wake up until later than usual	1

14. One night you have to remain awake between 4:00 – 6:00 am in order to carry out a night watch. You have no commitments the next day. Which ONE of the alternatives will suit you best?

Options	Score (please circle)
Would sleep only before watch	4
Would take a good sleep before and nap after	3
Would take a nap before and sleep after	2
Would NOT go to bed until watch over	1

15. You have to do two hours of hard physical work. You are entirely free to plan your day. Considering only your own "internal clock", which ONE of the following times would you choose?

Options	Score (please circle)
08.00 - 10.00 am	4
11.00 am - 13.00 pm	3
15.00 - 17.00 pm	2
19.00 - 21.00 pm	1

16. You have decided to engage in hard physical exercise. A friend suggests that you do this for one hour twice a week and the best time for him/her is between 10:00 – 11:00 pm. Bearing in mind nothing else but your own "internal clock", how well do you think you would perform?

Options	Score (please circle)
Would find it very difficult	4
Would find it difficult	3
Would be in reasonable form	2
Would be in good form	1

17. Suppose that you can choose your school hours. Assume that you went to school for five hours per day and that school was interesting and enjoyable. Which time would you prefer to start?	
Options	Score (please circle)
5 hours starting between 04.00 - 07.59 am	5
5 hours starting between 08.00 - 08.59 am	4
5 hours starting between 09.00 am - 13.59 pm	3
5 hours starting between 14.00 - 16.59 pm	2
5 hours starting between 17.00 pm - 03.59 am	1
18. At what time of the day do you think that you reach your 'feeling best' peak?	
Options	Score (please circle)
05.00 - 07.59 am	5
08.00 - 09.59 am	4
10.00 am - 16.59 pm	3
17.00 - 21.59 pm	2
10.00 pm - 04.59 am	1
19. One hears about 'morning' and 'evening' types of people. Which ONE of these types do you consider yourself to be?	
Options	Score (please circle)
Definitely a 'morning' type	6
Rather a 'morning' type than an 'evening' type	4
Rather more an 'evening' type than a 'morning' type	2
Definitely an 'evening' type	1

Scoring and interpreting this questionnaire

This questionnaire has 19 questions and for each question you will have circled a score on the right hand side. Your first task is to add up all of the points on the right-hand side from each question and write the total in the box below. For example, if you circled 2 for all of the statements, your total score would be 38. Total scores can range from 16 to 86, therefore, your total score should fall within that range.

/86

16-30	31-41	42-58	59-69	70-86
Definite evening type	Moderate evening type	Intermediate type	Moderate morning type	Definite morning type

You should now have a better idea of the type of person you are with respect to your chronotype.

You can complete this section by filling in the below sentence:

I am a(n) _____ type, and therefore I should make my decisions in the _____.

School of thought 1: We should align our decision-making with our chronotype

As mentioned in the introduction, there are two competing schools of thought which attempt to identify when we should make key decisions. The first school of thought suggests that we should align our decisions with our chronotype (i.e., morning types making decisions in the morning and evening types making decisions in the evening). Facer-Childs and Brandstaetter (2015) explored the effect of training according to chronotype on elite athlete performance. The authors' main finding was that peak performance differed according to which chronotype the person belongs to (Leone, Slezak, Golombek & Sigman, 2017).

- Early risers (morning types) were found to peak at 12:00pm

- Intermediates (neither one nor the other) were found to peak just before 16:00pm

- Late types (evening types) were found to peak just after 20:00pm

The authors also demonstrated that by aligning their decisions with their chronotype (performing at their individual optimal ToD), athletes improved their decision-making by up to 26% (Facer-Childs & Brandstaetter, 2015). This suggests that being aware of our chronotype can allow us to tailor the ToD we complete important tasks and make important decisions, potentially resulting in much more effective decision-making. Therefore, consider this in relation to the above questionnaire – are you a morning person, an evening person or intermediate? If you are a morning person, perhaps making your important FPL decisions just before lunch would be optimal. However, if you are an evening person, perhaps the best ToD to make your important decisions would be after dinner.

It is worth noting that this is a very simplified summary and interpretation of the research paper by Facer-Childs and Brandstaetter (2015). If you are interested in a more detailed account of their research, I recommend reading their full article, found in the references.

School of thought 2:
We should make decisions in the morning

In an experiment by Leone et al. (2017), the effect of ToD was explored specifically in relation to decision-making, represented by online chess. For those of you that are unaware, Norwegian chess grandmaster Magnus Carlsen is a consistently top manager in FPL, finishing 10th in the world in 2019/20. He claims that there are many similarities between chess and FPL, namely the ability to think several steps ahead. As such, this is a perfect study to explore.

In this experiment, participants had to have played at least 2,000 online games. Over 100 participants took part in the experiment and completed the Morning-Eveningness Questionnaire (MEQ; Horne & Östberg, 1976) that you completed above in order to assess their chronotype.

Here is what the authors found: "We found that players changed their decision-making policy throughout the day: players decide faster and less accurately as the day progresses, reaching a plateau early in the afternoon. This effect was observed for all players regardless of their chronotype, indicating that changes in decision time are mainly determined by the time of the day." The authors continue to say that: "Our results show that players play more accurately and slower in the morning, which could be interpreted as a strategy based on safety (prevention focus), and they play faster and less accurately in the evening, which could be a more risky way of playing (promotion focus)" (Leone et al., 2017, p. 53). They found all of the above, irrespective of chronotype.

Therefore, this research (unlike the previous school of thought) suggests that it does not matter whether you are a morning person or an evening person. Instead, it is the absolute ToD which is important (as opposed to chronotype). They do not suggest that one is better than the other (i.e., morning over evening), they simply suggest that morning decisions tend to be safer and preventative, whereas evening decisions tend to be riskier and attacking in nature.

However, they continue to explore the reasoning for riskier decision-making in the evening, which they attribute to **sleep pressure**. This theory suggests that throughout our wake cycle, the drive and desire to sleep slowly accumulates, resulting in the gradual degradation of our cognitive functioning (Schmidt, Collette, Cajochen, & Peigneux, 2007). In other words, by the time we reach the final few hours before sleep, our cognitive functioning is inferior to what it was earlier in the day. Once we consider this as the explanation for the riskier strategies chosen at night, it suggests that it may be ineffective and potentially detrimental to make FPL-related decisions in the evening (irrespective of your chronotype).

The effect of sleep and sleep deprivation on decision-making

As well as the effect of ToD on decision-making, we must consider the influence of sleep and perhaps more importantly, sleep deprivation (i.e., lack of sleep), on decision-making. The majority of research in this field suggests that sleep deprivation is highly detrimental when making important decisions. However, it is important to consider *how* and *why* sleep deprivation has this effect.

Harrison and Horne (2000) demonstrate that sleep deprivation impairs decision-making involving: the unexpected, innovation, revising plans, competing distraction and effective communication. Any decisions which require these elements are likely to be negatively affected by a lack of sleep. Further, there is a large cohort of literature which supports the role of sleep in aiding our ability to 'flexibly' make and adapt decisions (Harrison & Horne, 1999; Whitney et al., 2015). Overall, this research highlights that when we are deprived of sleep we are ineffective at updating our plans and considering new information – whereas good quality and quantity of sleep will improve our ability to flexibly adapt and make more effective decisions. Being able to plan and adapt to the unexpected, be innovative in our choices and flexibly revise our plans according to incoming news is critical to successful and effective decision-making in FPL – and sleep is critical to the effective execution of this.

As well as the aforementioned negatives, sleep deprivation is associated with increased riskiness in decision-making, in a similar fashion to decisions made in the evening. Following 23 hours of sleep deprivation, McKenna, Dickinson, Orff and Drummond (2007) found that participants were significantly more willing to take risks than they ordinarily would when there was the opportunity for gain. In other words, they were much more likely to attack the decision and less considerate of the possible downside. This is perfectly applicable to FPL, as often one of the key considerations is whether to attack the gameweek directly in front of us, or be more considerate of upcoming fixtures and potential blank and double gameweeks.

A perfect example of this was toward the back end of the 2020/21 FPL season, when Manchester United received the first triple gameweek in 15 years (GW35), but as a result had a blank gameweek directly afterward (GW36). Therefore, the key decision was whether to load up on Manchester United players at the possible expense of our team in GW36. The above research on sleep deprivation suggests that if we had a small amount of sleep prior to making this decision, we would have been more likely to attack the decision and less considerate of potential issues in the future. In other words, we would have had a Manchester United triple-up and worried about GW36 later down the line! Thus, you can see how sleep deprivation could potentially be quite detrimental in FPL if it is not mediated by strategic planning.

Conclusions and FPL advice related to sleep and ToD

As with most research, there are many different theories and findings about whether chronotype, absolute ToD, or both are important in decision-making. However, based on the large cohort of research and my own personal outlook, here are some important take home messages that you can apply to decision-making in FPL.

1. Make sure you get a large quantity of sleep. The importance of sleep cannot be overstated. Sleep is positively correlated to happiness, mental health, physical health (e.g., lower risk of cardiovascular disease,

obesity, stroke and cancer), improved recovery rates, attractiveness, longevity of life (Walker, 2018) and, at the very least, will improve our ability to update and revise plans (cognitive flexibility), which is critical to effective decision-making.

2. Avoid making decisions when you are sleep deprived. If you cannot increase the quality/quantity of sleep and suffer from sleep deprivation, my advice would be to make decisions when you feel least sleep deprived. If this is the morning, make your key decisions here. If you feel fatigued and tired in the mornings, make your decisions later in the day.

3. Make decisions (but do NOT confirm them) at the relevant ToD for your desired outcome. While the research on the best ToD to make decisions is conflicting, most research in gaming and gambling suggests that riskier decisions are made at night and safer, preventative decisions are made in the morning (e.g., Leone et al., 2017). As such, you may be able to tailor the times you make decisions based on the outcome you desire. If you need a rank rise and an attacking move, perhaps consider your options in the evening. If you need to prevent taking hits and want to protect your rank, consider your options in the morning/afternoon.

4. Confirm your transfers in the morning. While you can consider and plan your decisions in the evening to increase the risky/attacking nature of your decisions, the impact of sleep pressure and sleep deprivation would prevent me from advising you to confirm these decisions in the evening. It may be that a decision that appears to be a clever differential decision in the evening, will be perceived as a massive mistake when you have slept and are, therefore, able to update and revise your plan.

As a final remark on the topic of ToD and sleep, I advise you to make the decisions that feel most applicable to your own situation. While it may be that many people make poor/risky decisions in the evening, it may be that this is the time you function most efficiently and, therefore, you should continue to make decisions at this time. FPL is an individualistic and personalised game, and we must do what we can to enjoy the process. If this means making decisions at times when you are less cognitively effective, then so be it! If you are enjoying the game, then I believe you are playing it the right way.

End of chapter material: FPL decision-making timelog

As well as the self-report measure of chronotype in the form of morningness-eveningness questionnaire, another good way to find out when your decision-making is optimal is via a timelog. Simply, this is a method of tracking the ToD that you make specific decisions and then evaluating the quality of that decision. Importantly, we must be careful not to only judge the decision according to the outcome (outcome bias) and, therefore, it may be worth assessing the decision according to a number of markers. You can use the table below as a template.

ToD of the decision	Content of the decision	Evaluation of the decision one hour before deadline	Evaluation of the decision directly after the outcome	Evaluation two days after
E.g. 22:30	E.g. transfer out Salah for KDB to captain against Newcastle.	E.g. I feel as though I may have made a rash decision, but am happy enough.	E.g. KDB received 2 points and Salah received 9 points. Absolutely fuming.	E.g. Upon reflection, switching a premium asset on penalties to another the night before deadline probably was not wise.

Chapter 9:
Decision-making in the context of transfers and captaincy

This next chapter will explore the *nitty gritty* of FPL, where our cognitive biases can actually affect the explicit decision-making process, specifically in relation to transfer and captaincy decisions. There are a large amount of cognitive biases at play here, bigger than any other of the sub-groups.

To hold or to sell, that is the question...

One of the hardest decisions we make in FPL is whether to hold a player for the upcoming gameweek, or sell that player for another asset. In fact, 2019/20 FPL champion Joshua Bull admitted that one of his main tactics for success was to focus on removing players that he no longer wanted, as opposed to focusing on bringing in 'shiny new toys'. Often, the most difficult version of this decision is when you have an under-performing premium asset that is failing to return while the other premium options are consistently scoring. This is made even worse as often our premium assets are our captaincy choices. Therefore, can we use psychology to advise us when to sell our assets? I believe the answer is yes.

I will begin with two concepts that are very closely related and represent a similar point in relation to FPL: the **endowment effect** and the **mere ownership effect**. The endowment effect is defined as the circumstance in which individuals place higher value on an object that they already own, than the value they would place on that same object if they did not own it (Thaler, 1980). In one of the most famous experiments, Kahneman, Knetsch and Thaler (1990) gave participants a mug and then offered them a chance to sell it or trade it for an equally valued alternative (i.e., pens). The authors discovered that once the participants owned the mug, the compensation they required (willingness to accept) was approximately double what they were willing to pay to own the mug to begin with (willingness to pay). In other words, they valued the mug to a much higher extent when they owned it.

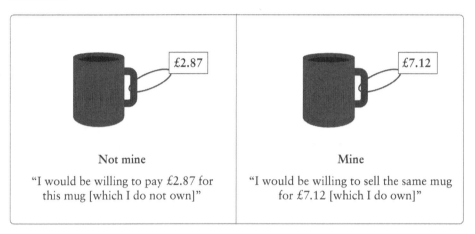

Not mine	Mine
"I would be willing to pay £2.87 for this mug [which I do not own]"	"I would be willing to sell the same mug for £7.12 [which I do own]"

The endowment effect is closely related to the 'mere ownership effect'. In social psychology, this describes the circumstance in which people who own an object tend to evaluate that object more positively than people who do not (Beggan, 1992). For example, we may evaluate a piece of art in our house more positively than a visitor. While the two concepts are very similar in nature, there is a subtle difference between the two. The endowment effect suggests that we place a higher monetary value on an object if we own it and we are less likely to want to sell the object (eager to retain unless we receive a high offer). The mere ownership effect is focused primarily on the idea that we value an object more positively than non-owners. Therefore, the endowment effect is often used in behavioural economics and the mere ownership effect in social psychology. Nevertheless, for the purpose of this book, both concepts suggest that as owners of objects, we value them more positively and regard them more highly than non-owners. Do you see where this is going, FPL managers?

It highlights a very worthwhile consideration you should have when deciding whether to hold or to sell a player. Often, our desire to hold a player could be cognitively biased by our mere ownership of that player or, in a similar fashion, due to the investment you have already made (endowment effect). As a result, a good question to ask yourself is the following:

"If I did not own this player, would I want to transfer
him into my team?"

If the answer to this question is no, but you find yourself holding onto that player regardless, you may be experiencing the endowment effect/mere ownership effect. My advice in this situation (from a theoretical viewpoint) is to sell. Do not hold a player just because you own them. If you would not want to transfer this player into your team as a hypothetical non-owner, you should not feel compelled to keep them in your team.

Finally, a commonly discussed bias in the world of FPL is the **sunk cost fallacy**, which is actually borrowed from the economics and investment literature. Sunk cost fallacy refers to the tendency for individuals to be more likely to continue with an endeavour after investing time, money, or effort (Roch, 1995). It has also been associated with refusing to cut one's losses, or throwing away good money. In 1985, Arkes and Blumer demonstrated the sunk cost fallacy with a number of clever experiments. The most alarming and striking example is taken from a hypothetical ski trip (Arkes & Blumer, 1985). In the box below, you can find the scenario proposed to students from Ohio and Oregon college.

Sunk Cost Fallacy (Arkes & Blumer, 1985)

Assume that you have spent $100 on a ticket for a weekend ski trip to Michigan.

Several weeks later you buy a $50 ticket for a weekend ski trip to Wisconsin.

You think you will enjoy the Wisconsin ski trip more than the Michigan ski trip. As you are putting your just-purchased Wisconsin ski trip ticket in your wallet, you notice that the Michigan ski trip and the Wisconsin ski trip are for the same weekend!

It's too late to sell either ticket, and you cannot return either one. **You must use one ticket and not the other.** Which ski trip will you go on?"

- $100 ski trip to Michigan
- $50 ski trip to Wisconsin

According to the theory of costs and benefits, we would expect that all individuals would choose the more enjoyable ski trip - the trip to Wisconsin. Interestingly, only 46% of participants chose the Wisconsin ($50) trip. The authors concluded that the sunk cost of the Michigan trip influenced the decision the subjects made (Arkes & Blumer, 1985).

This most accurately applies to FPL when deciding whether or not to sell a player that you have owned for a relatively long time and perhaps one that you have money 'tied up in'. By this, I am referring to a player that has risen in price since you have bought them in and, as such, you would lose money if you were to sell and then buy them back again at a later date. Similar to the above, the best way to counter this is to distance yourself from your own team and look at the player objectively. Even if you will end up losing money in the future, if the player is underperforming and not someone you want in your team, it is best to unload them earlier rather than later.

However, there are numerous instances in FPL whereby keeping a player in your team may not be demonstration of the sunk cost fallacy and may instead by astute management:

1. You have kept a player during a rough patch of fixtures and their next run of games is particularly appealing.

2. You have a large amount of money tied up in the player and will want to transfer them in again relatively soon.

3. You have other areas of your team to use your free transfers on and do not want to take a hit.

Nonetheless, we should be very much aware that we are prone to suffering from the above biases and bear them in mind when looking to transfer players out.

Captaincy decisions

Captaincy decisions are regarded by the majority of esteemed managers as one of the most important elements of FPL, but one that is often attributed to luck. While it is true that there is a certain element of luck to captaincy decisions (as with most FPL decisions), I will attempt to convince you that there are certain cognitive biases that we can avoid falling victim to, in order to allow us to make the optimal captaincy decision each week. These biases are not aimed to directly improve the captaincy decision, but instead to remove the possibility of making decisions based on fallacies and biases.

The first cognitive bias is probably one of the most applicable to FPL and one that I have not seen discussed previously in relation to fantasy sports. The cognitive bias that I am referring to is **non-adaptive choice switching**. To introduce this bias, here is a quote from an excellent paper exploring non-adaptive choice switching (Marcatto, Cosulich, & Ferrante, 2015, p. 1):

> *"When a good decision leads to a bad outcome, the experience of regret can bias subsequent choices: people are less likely to select the regret-producing alternative a second time, even when it is still objectively the best alternative."*

In other words, after choosing an option and having a negative experience with that option, we are less likely to choose it again in the future, despite it potentially being the best option in the new scenario. We are almost holding a grudge against a particular option or decision. This aligns perfectly well with FPL, in particular, 50/50 captaincy decisions.

Imagine you are choosing between captaining Sadio Mane at home to a leaky Sheffield United defence, or Raheem Sterling away at Chelsea who are sitting in 2nd place. You choose Mane. Liverpool win 4-0 but Mane hits the post and has a shot cleared off the line to earn you 3 points. Alternatively, Man City draw with Chelsea but Sterling scores from 6 yards out to pick up 9 points with bonus.

Most probably, Mane was the best captaincy decision. However, you are left incredibly frustrated with his blank as other people captained Sterling. Next month, Mane faces Southampton at home, who have the worst defensive record in the league and injuries to 3 of their starting 4 defenders. Non-adaptive choice switching would suggest that due to the negative and regretful experience in the prior gameweek, we may avoid captaining Mane again, despite him being the best option on paper.

The important thing here is that we should *not* let emotional regret from a previous decision influence future decisions. I have often seen people state things such as: "I will not captain Son again as last time I captained him he was sent off". Realistically, that prior event should not influence your decision when choosing captaincy for an upcoming gameweek. Instead, the focus should be on form, statistics, eye test and gut feeling. Attempt to not bias your decision-making with past negative events.

Psychology borrowed from the gambling literature

The final bias worth discussing here is borrowed from the gambling literature and applies to both transfer and captaincy decisions. This bias is termed the **gambler's fallacy**. The backstory for the gambler's fallacy is actually a very interesting one. In 1913, one of the casinos in Monte Carlo took millions off of several of the best roulette players in the world in the space of only a few hours. For those of you that do not play roulette, you can bet on a single number from 1 to 36 (more often than not 0 too), or bet on a grouping such as odd vs. even, or black vs. red. A wheel is then spun in one direction and the ball is spun in the opposite direction, until it lands on a number.

On this famous night in Monte Carlo, the ball landed on a black number 26 times in a row. That is the equivalent of flipping a coin and it landing on heads 26 times in a row. After approximately 10 black showings in a row, the gamblers began to place larger and larger amounts of money on red, said to be thinking: 'Surely red will eventually come up after all of these black showings'. In other words, they believed that the more times the black came up in a row, the more likely it would be that red would show on the next spin. Every time black showed up again, more gamblers began betting large amounts on red, convinced that red was 'due' to show up. This is, of course, incorrect.

To explain this, it is important to understand that each spin is independent of the other spins. In the example of a coin flip, each flip is completely independent of the previous flip and future flips. No matter what the previous flips resulted in, the new flip will always be a 50/50 chance between heads and tails. In roulette, therefore, the previous black showings did not influence future spins – it is always a 50/50 chance that it will land on red or black.

Therefore, the gambler's fallacy is the false belief that an upcoming random event (e.g., a new roulette spin) is more or less likely to occur as a result of previous random events (e.g., consecutive black roulette spins) (Ayton & Fischer, 2004). In FPL, this can apply to both captaincy decisions and the decision to sell a player. In particular, it can often be applied when a premium asset with an otherwise consistent history blanks two games in a row – take Marcus Rashford as a hypothetical example. In this example,

Rashford has blanked three games in a row while other premium assets are performing very well. If you stuck with Rashford throughout those three games, you may be thinking to yourself: "I will keep him, because he is **due** a haul." I urge you *not* to think in this frame of mind. In football in particular, using the word 'due' can be very dangerous.

Just because Rashford blanked in his previous two games does *not* make him more likely to return in the upcoming games. The upcoming games should be viewed separately to the previous games. The only reason you should use past games is for eye tests and underlying statistics. That is, if Rashford had excellent underlying statistics in the previous three games and was, therefore, 'unlucky' not to return, you can at that stage predict with a touch more evidence that he 'could' do well in the upcoming games. However, simply keeping a premium asset because they blanked in the last few games and they are normally quite consistent, is not a psychologically or statistically valid method of decision-making and, therefore, I urge you not to take this approach. If a player is blanking in consecutive games, it is potentially indicative that it is time to sell that player, rather than blindly hoping that they are due a return.

Chapter 10:
The psychology of being a fan

Own club bias

The last consideration that we should have when making important decisions in FPL is the effect of being a supporter. This will be one of the shorter chapters in the book, but without doubt deserves it's own section. As FPL managers, the large majority of us will love the game of football first and foremost, and part of this will include the following and passionate support of a football club. While some of you reading this will support teams from other countries or the lower leagues of English football, the vast majority will support a team from the Premier League, or at the very least have a preference for some clubs and a dislike for other clubs.

As part of being a supporter, we are prone to having exaggerated positive or negative views towards players from our own clubs. Indeed, due to the high likelihood of individuals being heavily emotionally biased toward the team they support, there has been a large amount of research into fandom behaviour in the field of social psychology. Specifically, two terms have been developed to explain fandom behaviour, BIRGing and CORFing.

Basking In Reflected Glory (BIRGing) is a self-serving cognition whereby we associate ourselves more heavily with our supported clubs when they are winning, so much so that the club's success becomes our own accomplishment. This was demonstrated by Cialdini et al. (1976) in a classic study on college students (university students in the U.S.). The authors found that the students were more likely to wear their college colours and apparel when the football team was victorious in their prior game and also were more likely to use the pronoun 'we' rather than 'they'.

In other words, they absorbed the team's victory as their own. The opposite of BIRGing is **Cutting Off Reflected Failure** (CORFing), which is a self-serving cognition whereby we cut off relations and ties to our club when they lose (especially in an embarrassing fashion), as we do not want to be considered failures (Dwyer, Achen & Lupinek, 2016). In the Cialdini et al. (1976) study, when the football team was unsuccessful in their prior game, the students were significantly less likely to wear their college colours and significantly more likely to use the pronoun 'they' rather than 'we'. In other words, they dissociated themselves from the perceived failure.

While not traditionally applied to FPL, it most certainly can explain the exaggerated emotions that we feel in response to players from our favourite club performing well (win-win) or performing poorly (lose-lose). When our team performs well, we want to embrace being a supporter of that club (BIRGing) and, as a result, may blindly and whole-heartedly look to get those players into our FPL teams.

The best example of this for me (as a Manchester United fan) was our brilliant run at the end of the 2019/20 season. *Did you notice how I said 'our' rather than 'their'?* After two games into this run, I was already on a Manchester United triple-up so that I could cheer my favourite club on and my FPL assets simultaneously. Essentially, we are able to boast about our favourite clubs performing well and how this has also translated to our FPL teams (win-win).

However, when our teams perform poorly we may often look to cut off ties to our club (CORFing), which may result in premature selling of our players – dissociating ourselves from the failure of our team and our FPL assets. In other words, applying the theory of CORFing, it could be that we are unfairly biased toward our players (sometimes) and, as such, hastily move them on after one or two bad results. Or alternatively, perhaps we are reluctant to buy players from our favourite clubs as we are pessimistic that 'it will not last, they will only let me down'.

Indeed, a recent study by Dwyer et al. (2016) demonstrated that BIRGing and CORFing behaviours were extended to fantasy football (NFL, American Football) – which confirms my hypothesising: "the results of the current study suggest that the social-psychological reactions witnessed in traditional team fandom were replicated through fantasy participation" (p. 152).

Therefore, it is wise to bear in mind our natural tendencies to associate ourselves with our favourite clubs when they are winning (buying and captaining our club's players) and dissociate ourselves from our favourite clubs when they are losing (selling our club's players)!

Chapter 11:
The 90 minutes following the FPL deadline

Often, one of the most difficult times in an FPL gameweek is the 90 minutes following the deadline. That is, when you have submitted your team and eagerly await the team news from the first game. It is also the time when people are posting their teams on social media. The combination of seeing lots of other great teams, and one of your players potentially not being in the starting XI is enough to ruin your weekend before it even begins.

My key advice driven by both research and experience, is to take a step away from the game and social media, and socialise or get some exercise.

Part of the reasoning for this advice stems from a cognitive bias known as the illusion of control (Langer, 1975). The **illusion of control** refers to the tendency for individuals to believe they have control over the outcome of random, external events that they demonstrate no ability to directly influence.

This is true for FPL in its entirety – while we can choose players that are in form, and make educated and well-informed decisions, the actual outcome of those decisions are completely out of our control. We are attempting to predict how 10 matches of 11 vs. 11 will perform, and have no ability to influence the eventual outcome of these matches. This illusion of control also applies in the moments following the deadline.

As a mantra during my bachelors degree, I used to say the following to my close friends:

> *"You get your grade the moment you put your pen down in that exam hall. There is no use in stressing after you have finished writing, as you now have no control or ability to change the outcome."*

The same goes for FPL and your gameweek, so here it is adapted for FPL:

> *"You get your gameweek score the moment you submit your team prior to the deadline. There is no use in stressing after you have submitted, as you now have no control or ability to change the outcome."*

As soon as the deadline passes, your ability to influence the eventual score that your team receives is non-existent. As a result, I advise you to detach yourself from the website and social media, and get a nice walk in with some family or friends. This will remind you that you have no control after the deadline passes, and hopefully help release some of the tension felt as you await the first game of the weekend.

P◆RT THREE

POST-GAMEWEEK REFLECTIONS

Introduction to Part Three

After the euphoria of a brilliant week, or the misery of a disappointing one, we must process how our team performed, reflect on the decisions we made and prepare for the upcoming gameweek, to repeat the cycle once again.

This process begins with an evaluation of the gameweek that has just passed.

Chapter 12:
Post-gameweek evaluations – how did I do?

As avid FPL managers, immediately after the gameweek ends, we look at our team performance for the week, check our overall rank, and assess where we did well and where we could have improved. However, within this post-hoc evaluation, we can often exercise two of the most well-researched cognitive biases in cognitive psychology: **outcome bias** and **hindsight bias**.

Outcome bias refers to the tendency to evaluate our decisions based on the eventual outcome, as opposed to the decision-making process. This is demonstrated quite strikingly in a classic study by Baron and Hershey (1988). Here, the authors gave undergraduate students descriptions and outcomes of decisions made relating to 15 medical scenarios. In other words, the participants were presented with the scenario, the decision to be made, and the eventual outcome of the decision. Here is an example of two medical matters that the participants were presented with:

Outcome bias (Baron & Hershey, 1988)

Medical Scenario A	Medical Scenario B
"A 55-year-old man had a heart condition. He had to stop working because of chest pain. He enjoyed his work and did not want to stop. His pain also interfered with other things, such as travel and recreation. A type of bypass operation would relieve his pain and increase his life expectancy from age 65 to age 70. However, 8% of the people who have this operation die from the operation itself. His physician decided to go ahead with the operation. The operation succeeded and the man lived. Evaluate the physician's decision to go ahead with the operation".	"A 55-year-old man had a heart condition. He had to stop working because of chest pain. He enjoyed his work and did not want to stop. His pain also interfered with other things, such as travel and recreation. A type of bypass operation would relieve his pain and increase his life expectancy from age 65 to age 70. However, 8% of the people who have this operation die from the operation itself. His physician decided to go ahead with the operation. The operation failed and the man died. Evaluate the physician's decision to go ahead with the operation".

Take a moment. Do you notice anything strange about these two scenarios? If you do, well done! In fact, they are identical scenarios with respect to the context, decision-making and likelihood of success. The only difference here is that in medical scenario A, the operation was a success and the man lived. In medical scenario B, the operation failed and the man died. In the actual study, participants were not presented with these scenarios back-to-back (there was a period of time in between), and therefore they were unaware they had already seen the same scenario previously. After being presented with each scenario, participants were asked to evaluate the decision on the following scale (from 3 to -3):

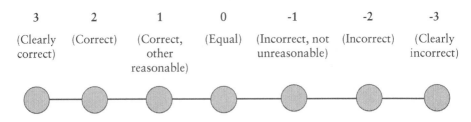

3	2	1	0	-1	-2	-3
(Clearly correct)	(Correct)	(Correct, other reasonable)	(Equal)	(Incorrect, not unreasonable)	(Incorrect)	(Clearly incorrect)

3 = clearly correct, and the opposite decision would be inexcusable;

2 = correct, all things considered;

1 = correct, but the opposite would be reasonable too;

0 = the decision and its opposite are equally good;

-1 = incorrect, but not unreasonable;

-2 = incorrect, all things considered;

-3 = incorrect and inexcusable.

Across the 15 medical scenarios, the authors found that participants rated the decisions as significantly worse (i.e., on the above scale a -2 or a -3) when the outcome was negative (medical scenario B) and significantly better (i.e., on the above scale a 2 or a 3) when the outcome was positive (medical scenario A), despite them being exactly the same scenario with exactly the same decision being made. That is, rather than evaluate the decision based on the logic and context in which the decision was made, they were unconsciously biased by the eventual outcome (outcome bias).

An example of this in FPL can be a simple captaincy choice. Imagine a scenario in which you are deciding between Mo Salah (playing at home vs. Newcastle) and Bruno Fernandes (playing away vs. Wolves) as your captaincy choice. In the last 5 gameweeks, Salah has 4 goals and 3 assists, Liverpool have won 4 of their last 5 games and their opponents Newcastle are virtually relegated. Alternatively, Bruno Fernandes has 1 goal and 2 assists, Manchester United have lost their last two games away from home and Wolves are fighting for a Europa League spot in the league.

As such, you decide to captain Mo Salah. Surprise surprise, Mo Salah blanks and Fernandes scores a brace with maximum bonus points to return a double-digit haul. The gameweek has now ended and you are looking at your team with the captaincy blank. The bias here would be to evaluate the decision based on its outcome. With only 2 points returned (4 in total with captaincy), you may view your decision to captain Salah in a harsh and critical light. However, the decision-making process was justified and due to the difficulty of getting decisions consistently correct in FPL, we must instead focus on the reasons we make decisions and the process that led to the eventual decision.

In other words, instead of being unhappy with your decision because your captain blanked (outcome bias), you should try to reflect positively on your decision because it was made in a sound and logical fashion. Not only will this hopefully improve your outlook on your decisions, it will also lead to more effective and accurate decision-making.

That is, by focusing on the process instead of the outcome, we can learn to improve our analysis and decision-making techniques rather than just responding post-hoc to points gathered in that gameweek (Lefgren, Platt, & Price, 2014). This links to the aforementioned 'illusion of control', in that all we can do as FPL managers is make the most well-informed estimations possible, but we cannot influence the actual outcome of those decisions.

As well as mistakenly evaluating the quality of our decision based on the outcome rather than the process, another cognitive bias we can engage in is 'hindsight bias'. Hindsight refers to the process whereby individuals recognise the key elements of a situation only after the situation has occurred. Therefore, hindsight bias refers to the tendency for individuals to believe an event was predictable after the outcome becomes known, also termed the 'knew it all along effect' (Roese & Vohs, 2012). It is believed to stem from a combination of aspects including memory distortion and subjective beliefs about one's prediction abilities.

Here are some common examples of hindsight bias that we see every day on social media platforms such as Twitter. As per earlier in the book, these are fictional tweets.

Mo Salah completes his hat trick against Manchester United.

I knew that he was going to do really well this week and that I should have captained him, but I was put off by the fixture and captained Danny Ings. Argh!!

I knew that Jesse Lingard would blank this week, even though he had an easier fixture. He was always going to regress to his underlying statistics

Of course, there is no possible way that any manager can accurately 'know' these things, as they have no control over the future outcome of a football match (once again linking to the illusion of control). It is also always very comedic that these tweets only start to surface after the game has been played. If we 'knew' it was going to happen, why did we not announce it before the match?

Very importantly here, I am not recommending that you completely disregard the outcome of your decisions in FPL and general life. Without using the outcome, it is difficult to objectively assess whether our decision was successful. Ultimately, the most objective measure of success at the end of the season is our overall rank, which is the direct result of how many points we score each week. However, as discussed by Baron and Hershey (1988), the issue arises when people overuse and rely on the outcome of an event to evaluate their decision. Not only will the overuse of outcome result in negative emotions when an otherwise sound decision does not result in actual FPL points, but it will also prevent you from improving and fine-tuning your decision-making process.

Chapter 13:
Psychological advice for coping with negative outcomes

This is perhaps the area of Psychology which is most important for the enjoyment of FPL. When things are going smoothly and every decision you make turns to gold, FPL is truly one of the best games in the world. However, due to the difficulty of achieving consistent success in FPL, every manager will be faced at one point or another with the feeling of disappointment, torment, or frustration; both at the game and at oneself. As such, it is important to be equipped with the appropriate tools to deal adaptively with these negative emotions.

I would like to draw your attention to something very important before we begin. This chapter contains very general advice that I hope you can directly benefit from taking into account. However, I am not a clinical psychologist, nor am I able to have a one-on-one meeting with you to tailor the advice to your specific personality, behaviours, and cognitions. Further, this advice is likely to only be effective to a certain point.

If you experience any of the following in relation with FPL, I advise that you seek professional advice and look to stop playing the game in the short term: tight chest; difficulties breathing; sadness and feeling 'low' over long periods of time (2 or more weeks) to the extent whereby it interferes with everyday life; loss of appetite and/or nausea; suicidal ideologies.

There is a website called Befrienders Worldwide (https://www.befrienders. org/) that can point you in the right direction for a form of support via telephone, SMS, messaging, internet chat or face to face meetings, depending on the country you are in. For those in the UK, you can call the Samaritans UK (phone number 116 123) to speak to someone immediately.

That being said, if you are sometimes negatively affected by FPL (but not to the above extent), and would like to be equipped with the tools to deal with that, look no further than this chapter.

Appreciate the difficulty of FPL

It is important to note from the start, that FPL is an incredibly difficult game, requiring both a great degree of luck and skill. We are trying to predict in advance how 11 vs. 11 humans will perform against each other over 90 minutes, for 10 games, every week! Assuming all of the teams use their three substitutions, there will be 280 players playing each week. We have to select only 15 of these, start only 11, and captain only one! Not only can we only select 15 out of 280 players, we also have to deal with largely uncontrollable events:

- Rotation

- Injuries

- Postponements

- Fixture congestion

- Poor officiating

- Freak incidents (e.g., own goals)

- Poor performances

- And many more!

Therefore, while we can do everything in our power to put the best XI out possible, the result of how our squad performs each gameweek is largely uncontrollable (illusion of control). There is undoubtedly a large amount of luck involved in FPL. So, cut yourself some slack – it really is a very complex and challenging game to master on a regular basis.

The importance of highs and lows

Positivity only makes sense because there exists negativity. Embrace both. This is a vitally important concept, and applicable to FPL for two reasons.

Firstly, without the experience of negative emotions, positive emotions will begin to become the norm. As such, the adrenaline, euphoria, and utter enjoyment associated with getting a decision correct in FPL will suddenly become less enjoyable. Without the lows, the highs just aren't as high! Secondly, negative events and 'mistakes' stimulate improved thought processes and help us move forward with a more positive world view (Vohs, Aaker, & Catapano, 2019).

A great quote to emphasise this is:

> *"Some of the best lessons we ever learn, we learn from our mistakes and failures. The error of the past is the wisdom of the future."*
> (Tyron Edwards)

Therefore, it is best to try to accept that lows are a part of both life and FPL, and to see them for what they are: great learning opportunities and an important counter-balance for positive experiences.

Placing FPL in the bigger picture of your life – self-distancing

Given the fact that you are reading this book, I will assume that FPL is not only a passion of yours, but something that you consider to be more than 'just a game'. As such, when people offer the advice "don't stress, it's just a game", we struggle to understand and take this advice on board. Therefore, instead of considering FPL as 'just a game', I advise you to attempt to 'self-distance' or 'psychologically distance' yourself from the specific negative event.

Self-distancing in this context involves mentally separating yourself from the immediate situation, and attempting to take a broader perspective - that is, to see the bigger picture (Shapiro, 2016). This line of research comes from the belief that often we are too 'psychologically and emotionally immersed' in the situation to reason objectively and learn from it (Kross, Ayduk, & Mischel, 2005). This difficulty to evaluate and logically reason with one's own problems is a widely accepted problem, and people often claim that 'it is easier to give others advice than to advise yourself'.

As a result, often we are able to provide friends and colleagues with sound advice due to our emotional and psychological distance from the problem at hand – that being, we are 'psychologically removed' from the situation

(Grossman & Kross, 2014). By this logic, self-distancing could and should, facilitate adaptive self-reflection:

> *"By enhancing a person's level of psychological distance from the self, we expected people to be increasingly capable of reasoning constructively about their own problems."*
> (Kross & Ayduk, 2017, p. 84)

Indeed, this hypothesis has been confirmed by multiple studies. For example, Kross and Ayduk (2008) demonstrated that in comparison to distraction methods (e.g., spending time with the family, watching a film, exercising) and self-immersion (e.g., dealing with the problem head on) methods, self-distancing methods resulted in both an immediate reduction in stress and a lower emotional reactivity in future situations. While distraction methods were as effective as self-distancing for the initial reduction of distress, self-distancing was much more effective at reducing the emotional intensity when the same negative experience occurred again in the future. This is because we are equipped to deal with future situations. Distraction methods will help take your mind off of the negative event, but will not help you overcome the negative emotions long term.

Advice on how to execute self-distancing

While many of us have become experts at social distancing across the past year with the COVID-19 pandemic, this section will attempt to help you become an expert at self-distancing. We now understand that research suggests self-distancing is one of the most effective ways of dealing with negative events, such as those experienced on a weekly basis in FPL. The question, therefore, remains, 'how can I execute self-distancing?' The main way to successfully execute self-distancing is through modifying the language we use when engaging in **self-talk**.

Self-talk can be defined as "dialogue [in which] the individual interprets feelings and perceptions, regulates and changes evaluations and convictions, and gives him/herself instructions and reinforcement" (Hackfort & Schwenkmezger, 1993, p. 355). In other words, this can be seen as our internal monologue. When assessing emotional situations, such as the negative events that can occur in FPL, we will often internally process and discuss them with ourselves, but in doing so, are very attached to the situation. Here are three things we can do to engage in self-distancing:

1. Change from I to 'he/she': when considering the negative event, imagine that you are considering the event happening to another person, in this case, John. Starting from the beginning, you can go through and internally process the situation. What has happened to John? Why is John frustrated? Why is John struggling to process the situation? What advice can I give to John to help him? This self-distancing can take time to get used to, but when used effectively, is a very successful coping mechanism for emotional turmoil.

2. Consider the future bigger picture: here, we are attempting to distance ourselves from the current situation, specifically with respect to the timeframe. This can either be used in unison with, or in replacement of, the above point. In one year time, will John (I) really care that he had a captaincy fail at the beginning of the 2021/22 season? In five years time, will John (I) be thinking about his triple captain fail in the double gameweek of the 2021/22 season? The correct answer to these questions is no! To help drive home this point and to help you in future situations, there is a very useful motto known as the 5 by 5 rule:

    "If it's not going to matter in 5 years, do not spend more than 5 minutes being upset about it."

    Essentially, once again the point with the 5 by 5 rule is to attempt to see the bigger picture, and detach yourself from the emotions felt in the present moment. Once you are able to recognise that this event will not be important in five years, you are allowed to give yourself five minutes to process the event, before attempting to move on and digest in a rational manner. To reiterate, these negative events will seem so unimportant in the future. They only seem so important now due to the intensity of emotions that humans are programmed to feel, and we are caught up in the here-and-now. Considering the future in this way, will help reduce the magnitude and intensity of the emotions we feel, in turn relieving the stress associated with decision-making in FPL.

3. How can he/she learn from this experience? Lastly, we can consider how the experience can be used as a positive, or part of a learning curve. This can be viewed both with respect to the actual content of the decision, and also with respect to the emotional experience.

For the former (content), questions such as: How can John use this experience to make better FPL decisions in the future? How will John make sure not to make this same mistake again in future gameweeks? For the latter (emotional experience), questions such as: How can John use this experience to better deal with poor decisions in future FPL gameweeks, and other aspects of life? Has John strengthened his 'emotional make-up' after having gone through this negative experience?

To finish, it is vitally important that after successfully executing self-distancing, that you consider everything in relation to yourself once more. That being, once you have managed to conquer your negative emotions through advising John, begin to remind yourself that it is indeed you that has been through this experience, and that it is you that has successfully overcome it. Here, you will feel a sense of pride and be able to apply what you have learnt for future gameweeks.

Demonstrate competence in another area of your life

Linked to the aforementioned self-distancing is this final technique – give yourself something else to be proud of. This should not be mistaken for a distraction technique – that is, I am not recommending that you go out and complete an activity to take your mind off of the gameweek. While that is successful for many, I personally believe that it is a very short-term fix. By distracting yourself for an hour while you play football or speak to friends, you are only temporarily dealing with the issue. You are not equipping yourself to deal with the problem when distraction techniques are not viable or inevitably end.

Instead, this alternative technique allows you to demonstrate competence in another area of your life and, in doing so, will make you feel less angry, ashamed, or upset about the incompetence you may have experienced in that specific gameweek. For example, during the 2020/21 season I experienced one of my worst gameweeks of the season, dropping from 110k to 210k the week after playing my wildcard. However, I was not at all negatively affected by the experience. The reason for that was actually this book! I had made fantastic progress with my writing and realised I was still beaming from a productive and exciting week in another element of my life – my writing.

Demonstrating competence in another area of your life will help in a number of ways. Firstly, it counterbalances the negative emotions felt during the FPL gameweek. You can imagine that if you tackle anger and frustration with happiness and pride you will at the very least remove the dominant negative emotions you initially felt.

Further, if you demonstrate competence in an important area of *your* life (i.e., family life, work), it is likely to put into perspective how little it matters to have a bad week in FPL. Of course, FPL is very important to us, but one or two bad gameweeks will *not* negatively affect us long term and being successful in another element of our lives helps to demonstrate that FPL does not dictate our emotions and happiness.

An FPL tool – find your own technique for coping with negative outcomes

While I do believe that the best tool (psychologically-speaking) to deal with negative outcomes is self-distancing, this technique will not work for everyone. Indeed, a key theme throughout the book has been to find your own style of decision-making and management, and to play your own game. This idea extends beyond decision-making to your coping mechanisms and, as such, I want to help each of you find the optimal technique to deal with those negative outcomes. In the table below are five possible techniques for dealing with negative emotions associated with FPL, along with the reasoning behind adopting it and some advice on how to best utilise the method. I strongly advise testing all techniques, to see what best suits you. Every time you experience a negative emotion associated with FPL, attempt a new technique. Do this until all techniques have been attempted and you can confidently confirm the optimal one for you.

Technique	How do you implement it in FPL?	Pros and cons
Catharsis An intense release and expression of emotions in a positive and adaptive manner, often through exercise.	Completing an activity that allows you to express your emotions in an adaptive and positive manner: • Going for a run • Boxing session • HIIT training • Going for a hike • Meditating • Ranting (without shouting) to a friend	**Pro:** Catharsis often involves exercise, which releases chemicals in the brain known as dopamine, norepinephrine, and serotonin. These regulate our moods and lead to feelings of positivity. In other words, as well as allowing an outlet for negativity, catharsis often leads to inherent feelings of positivity. **Con:** Similar to distraction techniques, there is often the risk that after engaging in the cathartic experience, that we will feel negative as soon as we return to the original problem.
Self-compassion Similar to the technique of acceptance, self-compassion involves accepting the negative emotion for what it is. Self-compassion, however, involves going one step further and extending the compassion you would show others, to yourself. Be kind to yourself!	"I am going to be kind to myself - it was a pretty tough experience and I am allowed to be sad." "I made some good decisions, I was just unlucky. I shouldn't beat myself up, I have done really well lately."	**Pro:** Extends to other aspects of our lives. Helps to boost self-esteem and allows us to learn to love ourselves. **Pro:** Allows us to accept and acknowledge the negative event, rather than running away from it. **Con:** For many of us, self-compassion can be difficult to fully engage in. **Con:** This would be classed as a 'soft' or 'indirect' coping mechanism. It is not guaranteed to lead to more positive emotions, in comparison to some of the more direct techniques.

Technique	How do you implement it in FPL?	Pros and cons
Distraction techniques Completing a task or activity unrelated to FPL which requires you to focus your attention, thereby distracting you from your worries associated with FPL.	Completing a task that has no relevance to FPL, in which your attention can be completely transferred away from the game. Some examples include: • Socialising with family • Painting your room • Cooking • Gardening • Writing	**Pro:** This can often be the most effective way to completely 'forget' about the game and take your mind away from your worries. **Pro:** It is often the quickest method for dealing with negative emotions. Quickly shifting your attention is very effective. **Con:** This is more often than not a very short-term technique. Due to the fact that you are not directly dealing with the problem, often after distracting yourself, you will return to the same problem you started with, still unsure on how to deal with your emotions. **Con:** You are not learning any adaptive techniques to deal with the problem. What about if the negative emotions are so strong that you cannot distract yourself?
Demonstrating competence in another area This involves attempting to deliver success in another important area of your life, normally associated with family or work. Focus your attention on something meaningful.	Demonstrating that while FPL is not going well, other aspects of your life can still be successful and flourish. Some examples are: • Completing a work project • Completing a painting • Beginning writing a book • Teaching your child to ride a bike • Learning how to cook your favourite dish	**Pro:** This combines distraction techniques and self-distancing, as it allows us to take our minds away from FPL, while being successful in an important area of our lives will also place FPL in the bigger picture. **Pro:** There is a secondary positive as we are successful in something important to us, thereby promoting productivity and success in other aspects of our lives. **Con:** If approached in the wrong manner (with frustration), we can risk bringing some negative emotions from FPL and projecting them onto other aspects of our lives (to avoid this, try to take a small break before beginning the new task).

Technique	How do you implement it in FPL?	Pros and cons
Self-distancing Self-distancing in this context involves mentally separating yourself from the immediate situation, and attempting to take a broader perspective - that is, to see the bigger picture.	Consider your situation in the third person. What would you advise him/her to do? Consider the bigger picture: "In one year's time, will I really care that I had a captaincy fail at the beginning of the 2021/22 season"? Consider your future: "In five years time, will I be thinking about my triple captain fail in the double gameweek of the 2021/22 season?" Consider how the experience can benefit your FPL decisions: "How can I use this experience to make better FPL decisions in the future? How will I make sure not to make this same mistake again in future gameweeks?" Consider how this experience will help you cope with negative outcomes in future gameweeks: "How can I use this experience to better deal with poor decisions in future FPL gameweeks, and other aspects of life?"	**Pro:** This is the most effective and adaptive technique for dealing with negative emotions. We can develop our skills over time, and in doing so, become more effective at responding to these negative events. **Pro:** It is a long-term solution, as we are identifying the problem and dealing with it, as opposed to running away from it. **Pro:** We improve our ability to help other individuals as well, due to the nature of imagining the problem from another person's perspective. In other words, we are improving our ability to empathise. **Con:** It can be very difficult to execute without practice, especially the ability to place our situation in the third person perspective. This does develop with practice for most, but for some it will continue to prove difficult. **Con:** The very nature of detaching ourselves from our current, intense emotions can be difficult. For some, this will unfortunately not be something they find easy to accomplish, especially very emotional and heated individuals.

Chapter 14:
Looking forward to
the next gameweek

We are at the final stage of the gameweek, before we repeat the cycle once again and begin meticulously preparing for the upcoming gameweek. So far in Part 3, we have evaluated and reflected upon the prior gameweek, dealt with any possible negative affect and must now look ahead to the upcoming gameweek. However, once again, we must consider how our expectations of future gameweeks can be cognitively biased. Here, we are not looking at specific elements of the upcoming gameweek (i.e., not focused on research), but more generally the expectations we hold regarding how positive or negative it will be.

The first mistake we can make is thinking in terms of certainties. Everything we do in FPL is uncertain, from attempting to predict line-ups, to choosing our captain and making transfers. Realistically, we do not know what will happen in the upcoming gameweek and cannot predict the players that will play or perform well with any real certainty (remember the illusion of control). This tendency to perceive an outcome as certain when it is in actual fact uncertain, is known as the **pseudocertainty** effect (Tversky & Kahneman, 1981). Understanding that FPL is an uncertain game will allow us to build realistic expectations of the upcoming gameweek and will also promote healthy appraisal and coping mechanisms if one of those uncertainties negatively affects our gameweek.

As well as understanding the inevitable uncertainty associated with FPL when forming our expectations of the future gameweek, we must understand the importance of finding a healthy balance between positive and negative expectations. It is important to view the future positively and optimistically, while not having unrealistic expectations of what we can achieve. Often as excited, passionate FPL managers, we can perhaps unrealistically expect each upcoming gameweek to be the best one yet. The **exaggerated expectations bias** is the tendency to expect more extreme outcomes than the ones that will inevitably occur (Hilbert, 2012). This can go both ways, with respect to unrealistically high expectations or unnecessarily low expectations. Importantly here, if our expectations are too high, we will inevitably be disappointed when this unforgiving game hands us a difficult week. Further, there is evidence that having exaggerated expectations is predictive of greater hindsight bias, as there is incongruence between the expectations and the outcomes (Schkade & Kilbourne, 1991).

Alternatively, we can view the future in a particularly negative fashion, known as **declinism**. Declinism is the bias whereby we view the future as inevitably destined to decline or fail. This is often coupled with the cognitive bias known as **rosy retrospection**, which is the tendency to view the past more positively than the future. While psychologically-speaking, if we view the future gameweeks as destined to fail we can only be pleasantly surprised, it does mean that we spend the majority of our weeks negatively affected by the game, or at the very least, not enjoying it to the fullest.

My advice for attempting to view the future gameweek in a balanced, healthy fashion, is to set moderately challenging goals, while being realistic in what you can achieve given your low control over the eventual outcome. Some very basic, objective goals could be one of the following:

"I want to achieve a green arrow this week, no matter how small."

"I want to achieve a gameweek rank inside the top 2 million."

However, be sure to remember that these are once again out of our control, so do not be too critical of yourself if you fail to meet these goals. Further, these types of goals are bordering on 'outcome bias', as we are aiming to evaluate our success based on the outcome rather than the decision-making process. Perhaps a more appropriate goal would be to enjoy the upcoming gameweek more so than the last! Most importantly here, do not set yourself goals outside of the realm of what can be realistically expected. For example, do not set goals such as:

"I want to hit 100 points this week."

"I want to half my rank in the next 2 GWs."

We should make sure to appreciate that FPL is a game of uncertainties and also set positive yet moderately challenging goals in order to keep our expectations realistically in touch with what we can achieve.

P◆RT FOUR

THE PSYCHOLOGY BEHIND YOUR CHIP STRATEGY

Introduction to Part Four

In this section, we move away from the weekly FPL cycle and begin to consider the season as a whole. That is, another element of FPL which requires attention from a psychological perspective is your longer-term psychological strategy, which is mainly in reference to your chip strategy. To recap, a chip in FPL is an opportunity beyond the usual scope of transfers and captaincy to give your team an advantage. In an FPL season you receive five chips which can only be used once each. These include: Wildcard 1; Wildcard 2; Free Hit; Bench Boost; and Triple Captain.

Wildcard 1: the wildcard gives you unlimited transfers and the ability to overhaul your entire squad. These transfers are permanent. The first wildcard must be used by the halfway point in the season (often gameweek 19, although this was gameweek 16 in 2020/21).

Wildcard 2: the second wildcard is exactly the same as the first, but can only be used in the second half of the season.

Free Hit: this chip can be used once per season and allows for unlimited transfers in a single gameweek. The 15-man squad of the previous gameweek then returns for the next deadline.

Bench Boost: all 15 players in your team contribute toward your total score for that gameweek, including your four bench players.

Triple Captain: rather than your captaincy score being doubled as per usual, when this chip is played your captaincy score will be trebled.

Chapter 15:
Wildcard and Free Hit

The first thing to consider in this section is whether there are any psychological theories or biases which directly influence the way we utilise our chips. While it is difficult to give advice that transcends the specific situation and context, there is one specific bias which, if avoided, could transform the way you deploy the Wildcard and Free Hit.

Putting all of your eggs in one basket

The key cognitive bias to consider with free hits and wildcards is **diversification bias** (Read & Loewenstein, 1995). This is the tendency for people to seek to increase variety when making multiple simultaneous decisions. That being, the tendency to avoid 'putting all of your eggs into one basket', and instead spreading the risk and diversifying your choices. This is especially common in defensive or offensive "triple-ups" from one club. I will give you two examples where this worked especially well for me. In double gameweek 29+ in the 2019/20 season, I tripled up on the Wolves defence as I saw their clean sheet potential as being the highest, and in double gameweek 24 of the 2020/21 season I tripled up on the Burnley defence who had two favourable fixtures. By being aware of the diversification bias, and in these instances disregarding it, I was able to attain 30 and 40+ points from the two sets of defences, respectively.

To put this into perspective, if you play a 3-5-2 or 3-4-3 formation you will have 3 defenders and a goalkeeper (four possible sources of clean sheets). If you are willing to disregard the diversification bias and triple up on a defence (or at least double up on two defences), you will be relying on a clean sheet from two teams. Alternatively, if you fall victim to the diversification bias you may be relying on 4 teams for clean sheets. While the risk is lower in the latter strategy, you are statistically less likely to get 4 clean sheets than 2.

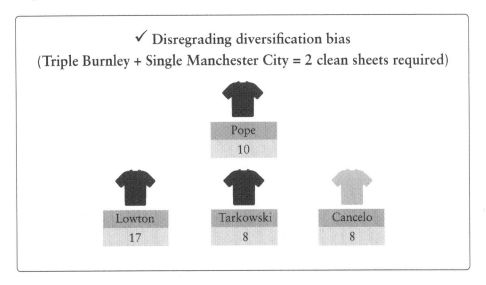

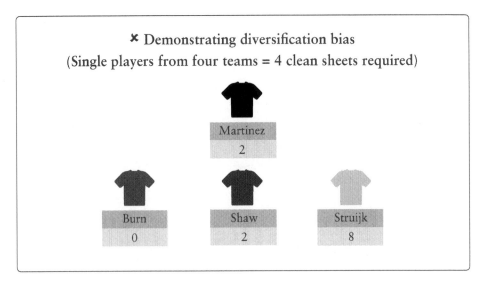

Therefore, do not be afraid to 'put all of your eggs into one basket', especially on a free hit. While diversification is more likely to result in a higher floor (likely to get points from somewhere), it is precisely the absence of diversification which can result in the highest reward.

Chapter 16:
Delayed gratification –
can you wait?

While the previous short chapter considered the actual decisions to make within the deployment of your chips, this chapter will consider when the best time to play your respective chip is. While there are many nuances as to when the best time to deploy your chips is in a given FPL season, the main two schools of thought are early and aggressive (e.g., Wildcard 1 played before gameweek 3) or delayed and methodical (e.g., Wildcard 1 played as late as possible to gather information and identify trends). While there are many merits to playing the chips early and attacking the weeks immediately in front of us, the reason that many will play their chips early is the inability to wait - they cannot delay gratification and hold onto their chips when they see potential opportunities early on. Here, **delayed gratification** refers to the ability to resist an impulse to take an immediate reward, and instead wait for a potentially superior reward in the future.

I am sure many of you would have heard of the 'Marshmallow Experiment' (Mischel, Ebbesen, & Raskoff Zeiss, 1972). In this classic experiment, individual children aged 3 to 5 years old were offered the choice between an immediate, small reward (one marshmallow), or two small rewards (two marshmallows) if they waited a short period of time. During this time, the researcher left the room and the child had to wait 15 minutes with the sweet directly in front of them. If they avoided consuming the marshmallow in the 15 minute period, they were provided with a second marshmallow. It is believed that this measures both self-control and the ability to delay gratification.

Since its publication in the early 1970s, there have been multiple criticisms of the original study. The most compelling argument is that social class (i.e., economic background) should have been considered. That being, for children from a poorer background, daily life delivers very few guarantees. There may be food one day and no food the next day, therefore taking the opportunity to 'cash in' on a reward immediately was probably the optimal choice (e.g., Watts, Duncan & Quan, 2018). Nevertheless, at the very least this experiment catalysed a large cohort of research and interest into self-control and the ability to delay gratification.

Why can it be difficult to delay gratification?

In the original study, it is easy to understand why the children may have struggled to avoid eating the marshmallow. As previously mentioned, the children were aged between 3 and 5 years old, and there is evidence which suggests that children develop self-control between the ages of 5 and 6 years old (Tao, Wang, Fan & Gao, 2014). Therefore, it is likely that the children in the original study did not have a fully developed sense of self-control. However, for us 'adults' playing FPL, why can we not avoid pulling the trigger and wait for a potentially better time to play our chips? Why are we so desperate to reap the rewards now?

The first explanation is once again cognitive biases, this time pulled directly from the field of behavioural economics. There are multiple biases and terms which explain our difficulty evaluating future rewards. There is a field of research known as **intertemporal choice**, which explores our decision-making across multiple time points. Research in this field tends to reveal that we are biased towards the present, in that we tend to give stronger weight to immediate rewards than potential future rewards (O'Donoghue & Rabin, 1999) – this is known as **present bias**. To further support this, research demonstrates that the further the reward is in the distance, the less value we place on it – this is known as **temporal discounting** (Frederick, Loewenstein, & O'Donoghue, 2002). Below is an example task from Callan, Shead and Olson (2011). Please take a moment to select the option you would choose if presented with the choice.

Temporal discounting task (Callan et al., 2011)
Which of the following two options would you prefer?
1.   £250 after reaching the end of this chapter.
2.   £1,000 in 365 days.

Unless you are in a position whereby £250 would make a very big difference now, the best value option is the £1,000 in 365 days. However, as this reward is in the distant future, it can be difficult to see the value of it. Therefore, perhaps we are cognitively wired to prefer immediate rewards to future rewards and there is very little we can do to fight that natural tendency.

The second reason is the generation and culture we have been born and raised into. Unfortunately, there is a great deal of evidence to suggest that we are part of a generation of impatience. How many times have you complained that your Saturday night takeaway was ordered over 45 minutes ago and it still hasn't arrived? Or complained that your internet went down 10 minutes ago and it still isn't working? Or that you have been on hold waiting to speak to an employee for almost 30 minutes? If you haven't done any of the above, I applaud you and perhaps you have very good self-control and the ability to delay gratification. For most of us, we have become accustomed to getting what we want within a very short period of time and waiting is often considered a thing of the past. As a result, when we are tasked with waiting for a reward (when we can potentially obtain a reward of equal value now), it is not something we are well-versed in given the modern day society. However, potentially this explanation is creating a negative outlook and possibly isn't the key reason that we struggle.

Another potential reason is the comparisons with social media. Touched upon in Chapter 2, there is a dark side to social media, especially in its ability to influence our decisions. As previously mentioned, we often see very extreme scores and extreme ranks on social media. For example, 100+ scores every week and managers breaking into the top 1,000 overall. As a result, we can begin to feel as though we desperately need to respond to everyone else doing well and feel the need to 'catch up' to those at the top. Therefore, we may rush into playing a chip that otherwise would have been better utilised later in the season. Social comparisons are always likely to make us feel like we could do better.

The final reason is potentially one that you have been thinking throughout this section – uncertainty, or the unknown. In the original marshmallow experiment, the children had a very clear motivation for delaying gratification (one now, or two in 15 minutes). With FPL – and most decisions in life – the reward in the future is far less certain.

That said, there is potential to hold your chips and avoid playing them early in the hope that there will be a better time in the near future. However, that superior time may potentially never arise, leaving you wishing you had played your Wildcard and Bench Boost weeks ago! This leads perfectly onto the next section – is it actually an issue to take the immediate reward? Are there positives to *not* delaying gratification?

Potential advantage of taking the immediate reward

This is a very important point to make, as thus far it may appear that both myself and the literature are suggesting high self-control and delayed gratification is always positive. However, that is not necessarily the case and there are definite advantages to taking the immediate gratification.

As we began discussing above, the major advantage to taking the immediate reward is that you can see directly what is in front of you. While you cannot ever confirm if the use of a chip is going to be successful, you can evaluate if it is currently a suitable time to use it. Unless there is a clear, confirmed double gameweek in the future, or a clear fixture swing, saving your chips for 'sometime later in the season' is full of uncertainty. In other words, while going for the immediate reward is sometimes viewed as a loss of self-control (i.e., no ability to delay gratification), it can often represent a rational action in cases where a future, superior reward is uncertain or unlikely. Therefore, if you are someone that tends to strike early and cannot wait to reap those immediate rewards, don't necessarily see it as a negative, not in FPL at least.

How can we improve our ability to delay gratification?

While it is difficult to categorically say whether an early strategy or a late strategy is best, there is evidence to suggest that at least acknowledging the possibility of delayed gratification could benefit you in FPL and everyday life. Whether you choose to accept a more immediate reward is ultimately up to you. Therefore, the key question is – how can we improve our self-control and ability to delay gratification? Or perhaps more notably, how can we improve our ability to recognise the possibility for delaying gratification?

The first way to improve our ability to delay gratification in FPL is through long-term planning. As previously mentioned, uncertainty is one of the main reasons that we may struggle to hold our chips and instead end up deploying them all very early. Without a clearly outlined plan of how waiting could result in a superior reward, why would we wait? Planning ahead and working out a point in the future where there is a strong likelihood that the chip can be used to produce greater gains than immediately possible, will give you more confidence in your decision to delay gratification. In other words, belief that there is indeed a potential for a superior reward in the future is a critical factor and planning ahead can give you that confidence.

For example, planning ahead may allow you to understand that despite there being an upcoming double gameweek (DGW10) whereby the Free Hit could be used, there will be a blank gameweek in the future (BGW18) that is likely to be a much better opportunity to deploy the Free Hit. Knowing that there is indeed a good opportunity in the future will make it easier to delay gratification.

The second technique to help improve your ability to delay gratification is by learning to exhaust all possible alternatives before deciding to take or delay the immediate reward. That said, if you are playing your Wildcard to prepare for an upcoming gameweek, is there another way you can prepare while saving the chip? If you are planning to Bench Boost, is there an alternative chip that would be better utilised, or perhaps no chip at all? Sometimes, if you consider the possible alternatives you will realise that the immediate reward can be achieved (or close to it) without the chip, or perhaps that the chip can be better utilised in the future.

Finally, very specific to Bench Boost and Triple Captaincy, is the actual benefit of the chip. Unless you are in a head-to-head league, an elimination league, or a cup of some kind, the timing of this chip does not matter – that being, the chip is successful by gaining you the most points possible, not by being played in a specific week. To put this into context, I often see comments on social media such as "I am going to use my Bench Boost chip to recover the -12 I took in hits", or "I am playing my Triple Captaincy to try to make up ground on my mini league leader".

While these strategies may increase your enjoyment of the game, or give you more confidence moving forward, ultimately they are not optimal thought processes. If you play your Bench Boost in gameweek 20 because you took a -16 and you score 24 points (negating the hit), or you play your Bench Boost in gameweek 37 for 28 points, the latter is ultimately the optimal choice for your overall rank. See the chip for what it is – not a way to pull you out of a rut or react to a poor gameweek, but a way to increase your total points at the end of the season.

P◆RT FIVE

CONCLUSIONS

Chapter 17:
My top five psychological tips

As we come to the end of the book, I realise that there has been a lot of information thrown at you throughout. Some of the information is critical, some is interesting and some may not influence your FPL decision-making or overall life. As a result, I thought it would be useful to reinstate the five most important tips and tricks to help optimise your decision-making, gain maximum satisfaction from the game and gain a psychological edge in FPL. You may benefit from creating your own top five list, almost your FPL commandments, based on what you have identified as most important to you throughout the book. Here are mine.

Tip One – Beware of the bias blind spot

As discussed in Chapter 1, the bias blind spot is the cognitive bias of recognising the impact of biases on the judgement of others, while failing to see the impact of biases on one's own judgement – we are blind to our own biases. Throughout the book we have discussed over 25 biases and, therefore, being aware that it may be difficult to acknowledge our own biases is probably the most important of them all. Continue to attempt to make yourself as aware as possible that you are also prone to suffering from these biases.

Tip Two – Consider the time of day at which you make key decisions

While it is difficult to advise a specific time for you to make decisions, it should remain at the forefront of your mind. I advise that you coincide your decision-making with your chronotype, which can be discovered by completing the questionnaire in Chapter 8. As discussed in this chapter, previous research has demonstrated that timing decision-making with our chronotype can improve performance by up to 26% (Facer-Childs & Brandstaetter, 2015).

In addition, regardless of your chronotype, there is evidence to suggest that decisions made in the evening are inherently riskier than earlier in the day, mainly due to sleep pressure. As a result, my advice would be to do your research and lock in your decision at the time of day that matches your chronotype and re-assess that decision the next morning before confirming. I have also chosen this as one of my top five tips as it applies to other aspects of your life, especially important life decisions.

Tip Three – Beware of the order in which you receive information

This tip focuses on being aware of the many biases at play in the order we receive information: anchoring bias, primacy effect, confirmation bias, plan continuation bias, semmelweis reflex and many more. Simply by taking in a specific piece of information before the rest, we can be prone to blindly sticking to that original plan, looking for confirming evidence, rejecting new evidence and, ultimately, failing to adapt to the dynamic game of FPL. Adaptation is one of the most important skills for a top FPL manager and issues with the order we receive information can negatively affect our ability to respond adaptively.

Tip Four – Avoiding outcome and hindsight bias

This tip focuses on the way you evaluate your decisions. Once a decision is made and we need to look back on it to assess its success, how should we do so? As previously mentioned, the focus should be on the thought process behind the decision, the research, the rationale. Judging the decision purely according to the outcome will not only lead us to succumb to outcome bias, but will also lead to difficulties with improving our decision-making. If we judge success according to how many points the player got, how do we improve for the next key decision?

In a similar way, attempt to avoid looking back on a decision and thinking "I knew that would happen". Not only is this incorrect (we cannot predict future football matches with any real accuracy), but it makes you feel like you made the wrong decision and will lead to negative self-evaluation.

Tip Five – Utilise self-distancing

My final tip is aimed at responding positively to bad gameweeks and, as a result, maximising your enjoyment of the game on a more consistent basis. We discussed it at length in Chapter 13, however, the key is attempting to place the poor decision and more broadly FPL, in the bigger picture of your overall life. If this is not effective, placing FPL in the bigger picture of your future life is normally even more powerful. By considering how small FPL will seem in the future, we can distance ourselves from the negative emotions we feel in the present.

Chapter 18:
Enjoy the wonderful game of FPL

The most important message in this book is: **enjoy FPL as much as possible.** If you fall victim to every single cognitive bias and continuously make suboptimal decisions, but you are having fun nonetheless – you are the real winner. Find a level of engagement that suits your everyday life, your career and your family commitments. Find a style of management which not only suits your personality, but also allows you to take the necessary risks to enjoy the game. Find the optimal amount of content which allows you to make informed decisions without making the decisions for you. Play your own game, but make sure that enjoyment remains at the centre of the decisions you make.

My final point is to consider why you play FPL. Whether it is driven by competition with your friends, or because of your love of the beautiful game, the main reason we should play FPL is for enjoyment – the overall rank at the end of the season should not be the focus. I implore you to be present in the moment. Enjoy the process, enjoy the good times, learn from the bad times, but remember to always be present and attempt to play FPL for the inherent enjoyment, not just the end outcome.

End of book tasks and practical help

In this final section of the book, there are some helpful structures and tasks to better optimise your decision-making processes. Remember you also have the questionnaires and tasks throughout.

Below are some further additions:

- An FPL diary that will help you avoid engaging in cognitive biases

- An FPL bingo game to help you identify the cognitive biases on social media

- A glossary of psychological terms

- A glossary of FPL terms

- Psychological references for studies and original papers

FPL diary to reduce cognitive biases (example)

Monday

1. What are your thoughts following the weekend football?

2. What are your initial plans, and why?

3. What decisions do you need to make this week?

E.g. Everton and Manchester United passed the eye test this week (GW15). I was especially impressed with Bruno Fernandes, who had three shots in the box and scored a brace. I feel like not owning a Liverpool defender could hurt me over the coming weeks, as they kept a clean sheet against Chelsea at the weekend, so that might be a priority.

However, I think that I want to roll my transfer this week, so that I can make two free transfers (FTs) next week. My main consideration will be whether to bring in Fernandes/Liverpool defenders, or roll my transfer.

Tuesday

1. What content/data have you consumed today?

2. How has this affected your decision-making?

E.g., Today, I listened to a podcast that outlined just how good Fernandes' underlying statistics are, especially at home. With his next two fixtures being Palace (H) and Newcastle (H), I am tempted to bring him in.

I need to compare the pros and cons of bringing in Fernandes this week, or sticking to the plan of rolling my FT.

Wednesday

1. What content/data have you consumed today?

2. How has this affected your decision-making?

E.g., Today I read a thread on Twitter which explained how Liverpool's defence is outperforming their xGC (expected goals conceded). Despite keeping a clean sheet against Chelsea at the weekend, their xGC was 1.98, and therefore perhaps they aren't as essential as I think.

I am worried of confirmation bias here though, as I would prefer not to bring a Liverpool defender in this week.

Thursday

1. What content/data have you consumed today?

2. How has this affected your decision-making?

E.g., Today I watched a YouTube video by my favourite content creator. He explained that his plan was to bring in Marcus Rashford, due to good underlying statistics, taking penalties, and a recent position change. I want to bring Fernandes in, and so I initially disregarded this information.

However, looking back through the cognitive biases, I am worried that I am displaying plan continuation bias/semmelweis reflex, by failing to consider Rashford as a good option moving forward.

Friday

1. What content/data have you consumed today?

2. How has this affected your decision-making?

E.g. Today I decided not to consume any content, and focus on my own team. Taking into account all of the data and the eye test, it appears that Liverpool's defenders are not a priority for me this week. I used multiple websites to compare Rashford and Fernandes, and they appear very close.

I have Rashford on my mind, but I believe this could be the result of the recency effect, in that the last piece of FPL content I consumed was the YouTube video praising Rashford.

Due to their closeness, I will be going with my initial plan, and gut feeling, to bring in Fernandes. I believe this is my intuition rather than plan continuation bias.

FPL diary to reduce cognitive biases (blank)

Monday

1. What are your thoughts following the weekend football?

2. What are your initial plans, and why?

3. What decisions do you need to make this week?

Tuesday

1. What content/data have you consumed today?

2. How has this affected your decision-making?

Wednesday

1. What content/data have you consumed today?

2. How has this affected your decision-making?

Thursday

1. What content/data have you consumed today?

2. How has this affected your decision-making?

Friday

1. What content/data have you consumed today?

2. How has this affected your decision-making?

FPL bingo – Cognitive biases edition

Just for a bit of fun, and to demonstrate how rife cognitive biases are for FPL managers, I would love for you to attempt FPL bingo for a full-week. Every time you see an account on social media demonstrate a bias; speak to a friend who claims they knew they should have captained X player (hindsight bias); or notice yourself engaging in a cognitive bias, you can tick it off. As soon as you have a row or a column (5 boxes), you can shout FPL bingo! Take a picture, tweet it to me (@MindGameFPL) and I will make sure to retweet it. Good luck! Some examples are:

1. Your friend tells you that he knew he should have captained X player (hindsight bias).

2. A Twitter account claims that they made a poor decision to transfer in an in-form player because that player blanked (outcome bias).

3. You find yourself seeking information which confirms a belief that you already had (confirmation bias).

Outcome bias	Sunk-cost fallacy	Belief bias	Exaggerated expectation bias	Law of instrument
Hindsight bias	Endowment effect	Narrative bias	Semmelweis reflex	Primacy effect
Confirmation bias	CORfing / BIRGing	Non-adaptive choice switching	Pseudocertainty effect	Clustering illusion
Mere ownership effect	Illusion of control	Framing effect	Diversification bias	Conservatism bias
Gambler's fallacy	Anchoring bias	Plan continuation bias	Recency effect	Bias blind spot

Psychology glossary

You could fill an entire book with psychological terms and theories, but here are definitions of the terms used in this book. While every attempt has been made to define the key terms in text, you can refer back to this if you need a simple definition.

Anchoring bias

The tendency for individuals to favour the first piece of information they learn on a given topic.

Apophenia

The tendency to mistakenly perceive connections and meaning between unrelated things.

Bandwagon effect

The phenomenon by which the rate of individuals adopting a point of view or belief is influenced by the proportion of individuals who have already done so.

Basking In Reflected Glory (BIRGing)

A self-serving cognition whereby we associate ourselves more heavily with our supported clubs when they are winning, so much so that the club's success becomes our own accomplishment.

Belief bias

The tendency to evaluate the validity of an argument based on the plausibility of the conclusion.

Bias blind spot

The cognitive bias of recognising the impact of biases on the judgement of others, while failing to see the impact of biases on one's own judgement.

Better-than-average effect

Sometimes referred to as illusory superiority, this effect refers to a cognitive bias whereby someone overestimates their own qualities and abilities, usually in comparison to fellow peers.

Catharsis

An intense release and expression of emotions in a positive and adaptive manner, often through exercise.

Chronotype

The propensity for an individual to sleep and function effectively at a particular point in their 24-hour cycle – simply put, whether they are a morning person or an evening person.

Clustering illusion

The tendency to erroneously consider the inevitable "streaks" or "clusters" arising in small samples from random distributions to be non-random.

Cognitive bias

The umbrella term used to describe the tendency for us to perceive information based on our own experiences and prior beliefs, which can result in distortion of information, unreasonable or inaccurate interpretation, and flawed decision-making.

Cognitive reflection test

A task designed to measure one's tendency to override a "gut" response and engage in further reflection to ascertain the correct answer.

Common knowledge effect

The tendency for group members to only share and discuss information that is common knowledge between multiple group members, and to not bring unique knowledge to the discussion.

Confirmation bias

The tendency to search for, interpret, and utilise information in a fashion that confirms, supports, and reinforces our already established beliefs and preferences.

Conservatism bias

The tendency to insufficiently revise one's belief when presented with new information. This can lead to the individual failing to react to the presentation of new information in a rational manner.

Correlation-causation fallacy

The tendency to mistakenly assume a cause-and-effect relationship between two variables, when there is in fact only a correlation between them.

Cutting Off Reflected Failure (CORFing)

A self-serving cognition whereby we cut off relations and ties to our club when they lose (especially in an embarrassing fashion), as we do not want to be considered failures.

Declinism

The bias whereby we view the future as inevitably destined to decline.

Delayed gratification

The ability to resist an impulse to take an immediate reward, and instead wait for a potentially superior reward in the future.

Diversification bias

The tendency for people to increase variety when making multiple simultaneous decisions.

Endowment effect

The circumstance in which individual's place higher value on an object that they already own, than the value they would place on that same object if they did not own it.

Evening type

A chronotype associated with sleeping in, staying up late in the evening, and being most productive as the day progresses. Evening types will often feel creative, imaginative, and productive in the evenings.

Exaggerated expectation bias

The tendency to expect more extreme outcomes than the ones that will inevitably occur.

Fear of Missing Out (FoMO)

The psychological term for the pervasive apprehension that others might have rewarding experiences from which one is absent.

Framing effect

The tendency for our decision-making to be dependent on how the set of options or data is presented/interpreted.

Gambler's fallacy

The erroneous belief that a specific random event (e.g., a roulette spin) is more or less likely to occur as a result of previous random events (e.g., previous roulette spins).

Group polarisation

The tendency for groups to shift toward more extreme decisions after group interaction, and also the natural inclination for groups to reach more extreme decisions than an individual.

Groupthink

A psychological phenomenon that occurs when the desire to maintain harmony within a community, results in the group failing to realistically appraise the idea and come up with logical alternatives.

Herd mentality

The process by which an individual's behaviour or beliefs align to that of the majority in the community to which they belong.

Hindsight bias

The tendency for individuals to believe an event was predictable after the outcome becomes known, also termed the 'knew it all along effect'.

Identity crisis

The circumstance whereby an individual's sense of who they are (identity) becomes insecure and uncertain, often in response to a negative situation or a large change in their life.

Illusion of control

The tendency for individuals to believe they have control over the outcome of random, external events that they demonstrate no ability to directly influence.

Intertemporal choice

An area of research which explores how and why individuals make choices about what and how much to do at multiple points in time - in other words, our decision-making across multiple time points.

Intuition (gut feeling)

An immediate reaction, feeling or preference, without conscious reasoning or analysis.

Law of the instrument

The cognitive bias involving an over-reliance on a familiar tool.

Maslow's hierarchy of needs

A theory of motivation which claims that human behaviour is driven by five needs: physiological needs, safety needs, love and belonging needs, esteem needs, and self-actualisation needs.

Mere ownership effect

The circumstance in which people who own an object tend to evaluate that object more positively than people who do not.

Morning type

A chronotype associated with waking up early, planning activities early in the day, and retiring early in the evenings. Morning types tend to be more alert in the morning compared to evening types.

Narrative bias

The tendency for humans to make sense of the world through stories.

Non-adaptive choice switching

After experiencing a negative outcome associated with a good decision, non-adaptive choice switching is the tendency to avoid choosing that alternative again despite it once again being the best option.

Outcome bias

The tendency to evaluate the quality of a decision based on the eventual outcome as opposed to the decision-making process.

Peer pressure

The influence exerted by a peer or group of peers on an individual to complete a behaviour or act that they otherwise may not have chosen to complete.

Plan continuation bias

The tendency for an individual to continue with the original plan, despite this plan no longer being viable after receiving new information.

Present bias

The tendency to give stronger weight to immediate rewards than potential future rewards.

Primacy effect

The tendency to remember items presented at the beginning of a list better than items presented in the middle.

Pseudocertainty effect

The tendency to perceive an outcome as certain when it is in actual fact uncertain.

Psychology

The study of mind and behavior. It encompasses the biological influences, social pressures, and environmental factors that affect how people think, act, and feel.

Recency effect

The tendency to remember items presented at the end of a list better than items presented in the middle.

Risk averse

A term used to describe individuals who tend to be reluctant to take risks, and would rather settle for lower risk, lower reward. Risk is normally considered unfavourable and unnecessary to these individuals.

Risk seeking

A term used to describe individuals who tend to accept greater uncertainty in exchange for greater rewards. Risk is normally considered attractive and necessary to these individuals.

Rosy retrospection

The tendency to view the past more positively than the future.

Self-compassion

Similar to the technique of acceptance, self-compassion involves accepting the negative emotion for what it is. Self-compassion, however, involves going one step further and extending the compassion you would show others, to yourself.

Self-Determination Theory (SDT)

A theory of motivation which claims that behaviours and social processes which foster autonomy, competence, and relatedness are more likely to increase motivation and enthusiasm.

Self-distancing

The process of mentally separating oneself from the immediate situation, and attempting to take a broader perspective - that is, to see the bigger picture.

Self-report questionnaires

A form of survey, poll, or questionnaire in which the individual is asked to read the question and provide an answer themselves without interference from the researcher.

Self-talk

Internal dialogue in which the individual interprets feelings and perceptions, regulates and changes evaluations and convictions, and gives him/herself instructions and reinforcement.

Semmelweis reflex

The tendency to reject new information that contradicts our already established beliefs and ideas.

Sense of self

Your subjective perception of your collective characteristics that form 'you' and who you are.

Serial position effect

The tendency for individuals to remember information presented at the beginning of a list (primacy effect), and the end of a list (recency effect), more so than the information in the middle of the list.

Sleep pressure

Throughout our wake cycle, the drive and desire to sleep slowly accumulates, resulting in the gradual degradation of our cognitive functioning.

Sunk cost fallacy

The tendency for individuals to be more likely to continue with an endeavour after investing time, money, or effort.

System 1 thinking

System 1 thinking is fast, intuitive, and reliant on emotional input, namely gut feeling.

System 2 thinking

System 2 is slower, driven by logic and reasoning, and analytical by nature.

Temporal (time) discounting

The tendency to place less value on rewards that are further in the distance.

FPL glossary

This is an extensive list of terms used both in the official game, on social media, and by content producers. Not all of these terms are used in this book, but this can serve as your FPL dictionary as you learn to master the game. If you are already a master, look away now.

Bandwagon

A term used to describe a sudden increase in popularity of a specific asset, often as a result of groupthink or herd mentality.

Bench Boost

All 15 players in your team contribute toward your total score for that gameweek, including your four bench players.

Bench fodder

Players that are very cheap and will likely never feature in your team, occupying the third position on your bench in most weeks. Also referred to as 'enablers'.

Blank gameweek (BGW)

A blank gameweek is a situation where some teams do not feature in that gameweek, usually as the result of matches being rescheduled due to clashes with domestic and European cup competitions. For example, BGW32 could be a blank due to Manchester City, Tottenham, Fulham, and Southampton not featuring.

Bonus points system (BPS)

Bonus points are a key part of FPL, and are given out in every game. The BPS utilises a range of statistics supplied by Opta that capture actions on the pitch, to create a performance index for each player. The players with the top 3 BPS in each match receive bonus points - 3 to the top performer, 2 to the second-best performer, and 1 to the third best.

Captaincy

In FPL you can choose a different captain each week, and this player's score will be doubled. You can set a vice captain for the situation whereby your captain does not play. If your captain does not feature at all, the vice captain's score will be doubled instead.

Chips

An option that you can apply to your team to make one-week or permanent changes, beyond the scope of regular transfers and captaincy. You have five chips: Wildcard 1; Wildcard 2; Free Hit; Bench Boost; Triple Captain.

Differential

A player with low ownership, usually below 10% overall selection (although sometimes considered to be below 5% selection).

Double gameweek (DGW)

A double gameweek is a situation where some teams play twice in that gameweek, usually as the result of matches being rescheduled into that week due to progressing in domestic and European cup competitions. For example, DGW26 could be a double due to Liverpool, Manchester United, Everton, and Wolves playing twice.

Effective ownership (EO)

Ownership that takes into account captaincy and benching. For example, if all managers owned Bruno Fernandes but did not captain him nor bench him, his EO would be 100%. If all managers owned Bruno Fernandes, all managers captained him, and none of them benched him, his EO would be 200%. If all managers owned Bruno Fernandes, none of them captained him, but half of them benched him, his EO would be 50%. If you own a player, but their EO is above 100% (and you have not captained them), any points they get will result in you receiving a red arrow, even though you own them.

Fixture Difficulty Rating (FDR)

Decided by the Premier League, the ratings of how difficult the upcoming fixtures are for a team, on a scale from 1-5. 1 (green) are the easiest fixtures, and 5 (red) are the most difficult fixtures.

Free Hit

This chip can be used once per season and allows for unlimited transfers in a single gameweek. The 15-man squad of the previous gameweek then returns for the next deadline.

Free transfer

Each week you get one free transfer, whereby you can remove one of your players (for another in the database) without the cost of points. You can 'roll' this free transfer (not use it), which will result in having two free transfers the next week. However, once you have two free transfers, you cannot stack any more. After using your free transfers, each further transfer will cost 4 points.

Gameweek (GW)

The term used to describe a round of Premier League matches, often referred to as a matchday in other sports and leagues. There are 38 gameweeks in a season.

Green arrow

A gameweek which has resulted in a rise in your overall rank.

Haul

A big score in a single gameweek, usually considered to be multiple returns. Many would say that over 10 points is a haul, others would suggest over 15 points.

Hits

The term used to explain a transfer which is not free - that being, it costs 4 points. A 'hit' is usually referring to a -4 transfer. Multiple 'hits' would normally be referring to a -8 or -12 set of transfers.

In The Bank (ITB)

This refers to how much money you have left to spend after making your transfers. For example, if you have £1.5m itb, it means that you can spend £1.5m extra when transferring out one of your players.

Mini-league

Private leagues that can be created among friends, colleagues or family. You need a code to join these leagues.

Money tied up

When you buy a player, you only gain £0.1m for every £0.2m they rise. In other words, if you buy a player for £10.0m, and they rise to £11.0m, you can only sell them for £10.5m. Here, you would have 'money tied up' in this player, as you would only be able to sell that player for £10.5m, but would need to spend £11.0m to bring them back in.

Nailed

If a player is nailed, they are likely to play 90 minutes almost every match. Ideally, we would only own nailed players in our teams.

Ownership

Usually reflected as a percentage, this is the number of managers that own a specific player in the database. Also sometimes referred to as 'Teams selected by', or TSB.

Out of position (OOP)

Players are categorised as defenders, midfielders, or forwards. Sometimes their classification in FPL is different to their actual position in real life. For example, FPL may class a player as a defender, but they actually play as a forward.

Premium players

A term used to describe the most expensive players in the game, usually over £9.0m or £9.5m in midfield and attack, and over £6.0m in defence.

Red arrow

A gameweek which results in a drop in your overall rank.

Set and forget

This is a colloquial term that can be used to describe a player you can put in your team long-term and not consider removing for any reason.

Often used to refer to goalkeepers that you can keep all season, or big hitting premium options.

Social media bubble (FPL)

The perception that social media is representative of a larger amount of the active FPL managers than it actually is, giving the impression that the information and discussions we see on social media are indicative of the general consensus across FPL.

Team value

The amount of money your team is worth, which can be ascertained on the official FPL website. Your team value at the beginning of the season is £100m.

Template

'Template' can be used to describe a player that features in a high percentage of successful teams, and in some cases the entire team in general. If you have an entire team of popular, highly owned players, your team could be considered to be 'template'.

Triple Captain

Rather than your captaincy score being doubled as per usual, when this chip is played your captaincy score will be trebled.

Wildcard 1

This is one of your five chips, which allows you to make unlimited transfers for one week, free of cost. These transfers are permanent and your previous team will not return. The first wildcard can be played at any point up until the mid-way point of the season.

Wildcard 2

This is one of your five chips, which allows you to make unlimited transfers for one week, free of cost. These transfers are permanent and your previous team will not return. The second wildcard can be played at any point in the second half of the season.

References

Abel, J. P., Buff, C. L., & Burr, S. A. (2016). Social media and the fear of missing out: scale development and assessment. *Journal of Business & Economics Research, 14*(1), 33-44.

Arkes, H. R., & Blumer, C. (1985). The psychology of sunk cost. *Organizational Behavior and Human Decision Processes, 35*(1), 124-140.

Atkinson, R. C., & Shiffrin, R. M. (1968). Human memory: a proposed system and its control processes. In Spence, K. W., & Spence, J. T. *The psychology of learning and motivation* (volume 2). New York: Academic Press, pp. 89-115.

Ayton, P., & Fischer, I. (2004). The hot hand fallacy and the gambler's fallacy: two faces of subjective randomness? *Memory & Cognition, 32*(8), 1369-1378.

Baron, J., & Hershey, J. C. (1988). Outcome bias in decision evaluation. *Journal of Personality and Social Psychology, 54*(4), 569-579.

Baumeister, R. F., & Leary, M. R. (1995). The need to belong: desire for interpersonal attachments as a fundamental human motivation. *Psychological Bulletin, 117*, 497-529.

Beggan, J. K. (1992). On the social nature of nonsocial perception: the mere ownership effect. *Journal of Personality and Social Psychology, 62*(2), 229-237.

Callan, M. J., Shead, N. W., & Olson, J. M. (2011). Personal relative deprivation, delay discounting, and gambling. *Journal of Personality and Social Psychology, 101*(5), 955-973.

Cialidini, R. B., Borden, R. J., Thorne, A., Walker, M. R., Freeman, S., & Sloan, L. R. (1976). Basking in reflected glory: three (football) field studies. *Journal of Personality and Social Psychology, 34*(3), 366-375.

Damasio, A. R. (1994). *Descartes' Error: Emotion, Reason and the Human Brain.* New York, NY: Avon.

Deci, E. L., & Ryan, R. M. (1984). The independence of positive and negative affect. *Journal of Personality and Social Psychology, 47*, 1005-1117.

Dwyer, B., Achen, R. M., & Lupinek, J. M. (2016). Fantasy vs. reality: exploring the BIRGing and CORFing behavior of Fantasy Football participants. *Sport Marketing Quarterly, 25*, 152-165.

Epstein, S., Pacini, R., Denes-Raj, V., & Heier, H. (1996). Individual differences in intuitive-experiential and analytical-rational thinking styles. *Journal of Personality and Social Psychology, 71*(2), 390-405.

Facer-Childs, E., & Brandstaetter, R. (2015). The impact of circadian phenotype and time since awakening on diurnal performance in athletes. *Current Biology, 25*(4), 518-522.

Frederick, S. (2005). Cognitive reflection and decision-making. *Journal of Economic Perspectives, 19*(4), 25-42.

Frederick, S., Loewenstein, G., & O'Donoghue, T. (2002). Time discounting and time preference: a critical review. *Journal of Economic Literature, 40*, 351-401.

Gonzalez, C., Dana, J., Koshino, H., & Just, M. (2005). The framing effect and risky decisions: examining cognitive functions with fMRI. *Journal of Economic Psychology, 26*, 1-20.

Gray, P. O. (2011). *Psychology* (6th ed.). Worth Publishers.

Grossman, I., & Kross, E. (2014). Exploring Solomon's paradox: self-distancing eliminates the self-other asymmetry in wise reasoning about close relationships in younger and older adults. *Psychological Science, 25*(8), 1571-1580.

Gupta, V. K., Saini, C., Oberoi, M., Kalra, G., & Nasir, M. I. (2020). Semmelweis reflex: an age-old prejudice. *World Neurosurgery, 136*, 119-125.

Guthrie, C., Rachlinski, J. J., & Wistrich, A. J. (2007). Blinking on the bench: how judges decide cases. *Cornell Law Review, 93*(1), 1-44.

Hackfort, D., & Schwenkmezger, P. (1993). Anxiety. In R. N. Singer M. Murphey & L. K. Tennant (Eds.), *Handbook of Research on Sport Psychology* (pp. 328-364). New York: Macmillan.

Harrison, Y., & Horne, J. A. (1999). One night of sleep loss impairs thinking and flexible decision making. *Organisational Behavior and Human Processes, 78*(2), 128-145.

Harrison, Y., & Horne, J. A. (2000). The impact of sleep deprivation on decision making: a review. *Journal of Experimental Psychology: Applied, 6*(3), 236-249.

Hilbert, M. (2012). Toward a synthesis of cognitive biases: how noisy information processing can bias human decision making. *Psychological Bulletin, 138*(2), 211-237.

Horne, J. A., & Östberg, O. (1976). A self-assessment questionnaire to determine morningness-eveningness in human circadian rhythms. *International Journal of Chronobiology, 4*, 97-100.

Janis, I. L. (1971). Groupthink. *Psychology Today, 5*(6), 43-46, 74-76.

Jones, P. E., & Roelofsma, P. H. M. P. (2000). The potential for social contextual and group biases in team decision-making: biases, conditions and psychological mechanisms. *Economics, 43*(8), 1129-1152.

Kahneman, D. (2011). *Thinking, fast and slow*. Farra, Straus and Giroux.

Kahneman, D., Knetsch, J. L., & Thaler, R. H. (1990). Experimental test of the endowment effect and the Coase Theorem. *Journal of Political Economy, 98*(6), 1325-1348.

Kahneman, D., & Tversky, A. (1979). Prospect theory: an analysis of decision under risk. *Econometrica, 47*, 263-291.

Kameda, T., & Hastie, R. (2015). Herd Behavior. In *Emerging Trends in the Social and Behavioral Sciences: An Interdisciplinary, Searchable, and Linkable Resource*, 1-14. Wiley Online Library.

Keaton, S. A. (2017). Profile 53. Rational-Experiential Inventory-40 (REI-40). In D. L. Worthington & G. D. Bodie (Eds.), *The Sourcebook of Listening Research: Methodology and Measures*. John Wiley & Sons.

Khatri, N., & Ng, H. A. (2000). The role of intuition in strategic decision making. *Human Relations, 53*(1), 57-86.

Kross, E., & Ayduk. O. (2017). Chapter Two - Self-distancing: theory, research and current directions. *Advances in Experimental Social Psychology, 55*, 81-136.

Kross, E., Ayduk, O., & Mischel, W. (2005). When asking "why" does not hurt: distinguishing rumination from reflective processing of negative emotions. *Psychological Science, 16*(9), 709-715.

Lamm, H. (1988). A review of our research on group polarisation: eleven experiments on the effects of group discussion on risk acceptance, probability estimation and negotiation positions. *Psychological Reports, 62*, 807-813.

Langer, E. J. (1975). The illusion of control. *Journal of Personality and Social Psychology, 32*(6), 951-955.

Lieder, F., Griffiths, T. L., Huys, Q, J., & Goodman, N. D. (2018). The anchoring bias reflects rational use of cognitive resources. *Psychonomic Bulletin & Review, 25*, 322-349.

Lefgren, L., Platt, B., & Price, J. (2014). Sticking with what (barely) worked: a test of outcome bias. *Management Science.* https://doi.org/10.1287/mnsc.2014.1966

Leone, M. J., Slezak, D. F., Golombek, D., Sigman, M. (2017). Time to decide: diurnal variations on the speed and quality of human decisions. *Cognition, 158*, 44-55.

Lopes, L. L. (1987). Between hope and fear: the psychology of risk. *Advances in Experimental Social Psychology, 20*, 255-295.

Lu, L., Yuan, Y. C., & McLeod, P. L. (2012). Twenty-five years of hidden profiles in group-decision making: a meta-analysis. *Personality and Social Psychology Review, 16*(1), 54-75.

Marcatto. F., Cosulich. A., & Ferrante. D. (2015). Once bitten, twice shy: experienced regret and non-adaptive choice switching. *PeerJ*, 3:e1035. https://doi.org/10.7717/peerj.1035

Margetts, T., & Butticè, G. (2019). *Fantasy Premier League: Unlocking the secrets to a top 1% finish*. Ockley Books Ltd / Monument Creative & Publishing Ltd.

Markovits, H., & Nantel, G. (1989). The belief-bias effect in the production and evaluation of logical conclusions. *Memory & Cognition, 17*(1), 11-17.

Maslow, A. H. (1943). A theory of human motivation. *Psychological Review, 50*(4), 370-396.

Maslow, A. H. (1966). *The Psychology of Science: A Reconnaissance.* Harper & Row.

McCoy, S. S., & Natsuaki, M. N. (2017). For better or for worse: social influences on risk-taking. *The Journal of Social Psychology, 158*(2), 1-13.

McKenna, B. S., Dickinson, D. L., Orff, H. J., & Drummond, S. P. A. (2007). The effects of one night of sleep deprivation on known-risk and ambiguous-risk decisions. *Journal of Sleep Research, 16*(3), 245-252.

Mischel, W., Ebbesen, E. B., & Raskoff Zeiss, A. (1972). Cognitive and attentional mechanisms in delay of gratification. *Journal of Personality and Social Psychology, 21*(2), 204-218.

Nickerson, R. (1998). Confirmation bias: a ubiquitous phenomenon in many guises. *Review of General Psychology, 2*(2), 175-220.

O'Brien, L., Albert, D., Chein, J., & Steinberg, L. (2011). Adolescents prefer more immediate rewards when in the presence of their peers. *Journal of Research on Adolescence, 21*(4), 747-753.

O'Donoghue, T., & Rabin, M. (1999). Doing it now or later. *American Economic Review, 89*(1), 103-124.

Östberg, O. (1976). A self-assessment questionnaire to determine morningness-eveningness in human circadian rhythms. *International Journal of Chronobiology, 4*, 97-100.

Pacini, R., & Epstein, S. (1999). The relation of rational and experiential information processing styles to personality, basic beliefs, and the ratio-bias phenomenon. *Journal of Personality and Social Psychology, 76*, 972-987.

Pompian, M. (2012). *Behavioural Finance and Wealth Management.* John Wiley & Sons.

Pronin, E., Lin, D. Y., & Ross, L. (2002). The bias blind spot: perceptions of bias in self versus others. *Personality and Social Psychology Bulletin, 28*(3), 369-381.

Przybylski, A. K., Murayama, K., DeHaan, C. R., & Gladwell, V. (2013). Motivational, emotional, and behavioral correlates of fear of missing out. *Computers in Human Behavior, 29*, 1841-1843.

Raafat, R. M., Chater, N., & Frith, C. (2009). Herding in Humans. *Trends in Cognitive Sciences, 13*, 420-428.

Read, D., & Loewenstein, G. (1995). Diversification bias: explaining the discrepancy in variety seeking between combined and separated choices. *Journal of Experimental Psychology: Applied, 1*, 34-49.

Roese, N. J., & Vohs, K. D. (2012). Hindsight bias. *Perspectives on Psychological Science, 7*(5), 411-426.

Roch, P. (1995). The strategic implications of sunk costs: a behavioral perspective. *Journal of Economic Behavior & Organization, 28*(3), 417-442.

Sadler-Smith, E., & Shefy, E. (2004). The intuitive executive: understanding and applying 'gut feel' in decision-making. *Academy of Management Perspectives, 18*(4), 76-91.

Schkade, D. A., & Kilbourne, L. M. (1991). Expectation-outcome consistency and hindsight bias. *Decision Processes, 49*(1), 105-123.

Schmidt, C., Collette, F., Cajochen, C., & Peigneux, P. (2007). A time to think: circadian rhythms in human cognition. *Cognitive Neuropsychology, 24*(7), 755-789.

Schwarz, N., Bless, H., Strack, F., Klumpp, G., Rittenauer-Schatka, H., & Simons, A. (1991). Ease of retrieval as information: another look at the availability heuristic. *Journal of Personality and Social Psychology, 61*(2), 195-202.

Shapiro, D. (2016). *Negotiating the non-negotiable: How to resolve your most emotionally charged conflicts?* NY: Viking.

Soosalu, G., Henwood, S., & Deo, A. (2019). Head, heart, and gut in decision making: development of a multiple brain preference questionnaire. *SAGE Open, 9*(1), 1-17.

Stasser, G., & Titus, W. (1985). Pooling of unshared information in group decision making: biased information sampling during group discussion. *Journal of Personality and Social Psychology, 48*, 1467-1478.

Stasser, G., & Titus, W. (1987). Effects of information load and percentage of shared information on the dissemination of unshared information during group discussion. *Journal of Personality and Social Psychology, 53*, 81-93.

Stevenson, S., & Hicks, R. E. (2016). Trust your instincts: the relationship between intuitive decision making and happiness. *European Scientific Journal, 12*(11), 463-483.

Tao, T., Wang, L., Fan., C., & Gao. W. (2014). Development of self-control in children aged 3 to 9 years: perspective from a dual-systems model. *Scientific Reports, 4*(7272), 1-5.

Thaler, R. (1980). Toward a positive theory of consumer choice. *Journal of Economic Behavior & Organization, 1*(1), 39-60.

Turkle, S. (2011). *Alone together: why we expect more from technology and less from each other.* New York: Basic Books.

Tversky, A., & Kahneman, D. (1974). Judgment under uncertainty: heuristics and biases. *Science, 185*(4157), 1124-1131.

Tversky, A., & Kahneman, D. (1981). The framing of decisions and the psychology of choice. *Science, 211*(4481), 453-458.

Vohs, K. D., Aaker, J. L., & Catapano, R. (2019). It's not going to be that fun: negative experiences can add meaning to life. *Current Opinion in Psychology, 26*, 11-14.

Walker, M. (2018). *Why we sleep: The new science of sleep and dreams.* Penguin Books: London.

Watts, T. W., Duncan, G. J., & Quan, H. (2018). Revisiting the Marshmallow Test: a conceptual replication investigating links between early delay of gratification and later outcomes. *Psychological Science, 29*(7), 1159-1177.

Whitney, P., Hinson, J. M., Jackson, M. L., & Van Dongen, H. P. A. (2015). Feedback blunting: total sleep deprivation impairs decision making that requires updating based on feedback. *Sleep, 38*(5), 745-754.

Wortham, J. (2011). Feel like a wallflower? Maybe it's your Facebook wall. *The New York Times.*

Zhang, D. C., Highouse, S., & Nye, C. D. (2018). Development and validation of the general risk taking propensity scale (GRiPS). *Journal of Behavioral Decision Making.* doi.org/10.1002/bdm.2102